M000093305

WILEY

Revenue Recognition

Rules and Scenarios

SECOND EDITION

WILEY

Revenue Recognition

Rules and Scenarios

SECOND EDITION

Steven M. Bragg

WILEY

JOHN WILEY & SONS, INC.

Copyright © 2010 by John Wiley & Sons, Inc. All rights reserved.

Published by John Wiley & Sons, Inc., Hoboken, New Jersey
Published simultaneously in Canada.

No part of this publication may be reproduced, stored in a retrieval system, or transmitted in any form or by any means, electronic, mechanical, photocopying, recording, scanning, or otherwise, except as permitted under Section 107 or 108 of the 1976 United States Copyright Act, without either the prior written permission of the Publisher, or authorization through payment of the appropriate per-copy fee to the Copyright Clearance Center, 222 Rosewood Drive, Danvers, MA 01923, 978-750-8400, fax 978-750-4470, or on the Web at www.copyright.com. Requests to the Publisher for permission should be addressed to the Permissions Department, John Wiley & Sons, Inc., 111 River Street, Hoboken, NJ 07030, 201-748-6011, fax 201-748-6008, or online at http://www.wiley .com/go/permission.

Limit of Liability/Disclaimer of Warranty: While the publisher and author have used their best efforts in preparing this book, they make no representations or warranties with respect to the accuracy or completeness of the contents of this book and specifically disclaim any implied warranties of merchantability or fitness for a particular purpose. No warranty may be created or extended by sales representatives or written sales materials. The advice and strategies contained herein may not be suitable for your situation. You should consult with a professional where appropriate. Neither the publisher nor author shall be liable for any loss of profit or any other commercial damages, including but not limited to special, incidental, consequential, or other damages.

For general information on our other products and services, please contact our Customer Care Department within the US at 800-762-2974, outside the US at 317-572-3993 or fax 317-572-4002.

Wiley also publishes its books in a variety of electronic formats. Some content that appears in print may not be available in electronic books. For more information about Wiley products, visit our Web site at www.wiley.com.

ISBN: 978-0-470-61948-3

Printed in the United States of America

10 9 8 7 6 5 4 3 2 1

CONTENTS

PREFACE

Revenue recognition is of critical importance to anyone in the business world, since it drives a large part of the perception of a company's value, which is reflected in its stock price. This in turn impacts the returns of investors and any earnings of employees that are tied to stock options. Given these pressures, it should be no surprise that the outer boundaries of revenue recognition rules are constantly being explored by company managers, which has led to the bulk of all cases of financial fraud.

Revenue Recognition not only provides a detailed view of the current accounting rules and regulations pertaining to revenue recognition, but also describes the exact sources of this information, how a company's treatment of revenue recognition is to be disclosed alongside the financial statements, and what policies, procedures, and controls can be used to enforce it in a consistent manner.

Revenue recognition rules vary not only by type of transaction, but also for some industries. Accordingly, the chapters of this book are clustered into transaction-related revenue recognition rules, and then into industry-related revenue recognition rules. Chapters 1 through 5 cover revenue recognition for transactions, including general principles, when collection is uncertain, when there is a right of return, and when there are multiple deliverables. These chapters include commentary about the revenue recognition positions of the Securities and Exchange Commission, as well as international financial reporting standards.

Chapters 6 through 13 then address revenue recognition for the following industries:

- Franchising
- Construction
- Motion pictures
- Not-for-profits
- Real estate
- Recording and music
- Services
- Software

Chapter 14 addresses a variety of miscellaneous topics too small for separate chapters, such as loan guarantee fees, sales with guaranteed resale values, advertising barter transactions, sales incentive plans, and so on.

This book is intended to be a source book for *all* aspects of revenue recognition—how to account for it, report it, and set up systems and controls to ensure that the rules are properly followed. Hopefully, *Revenue Recognition* will assist you in consistently recognizing revenue in the correct amounts, at the right time, and in accordance with generally accepted accounting principles.

Steven M. Bragg
Centennial, Colorado
March 2010

ABOUT THE AUTHOR

Steven Bragg, CPA, CMA, CIA, CPIM, has been the chief financial officer or controller of four companies, as well as a consulting manager at Ernst & Young and auditor at Deloitte & Touche. He received a master's degree in finance from Bentley College, an MBA from Babson College, and a bachelor's degree in economics from the University of Maine. He has been the two-time president of the Colorado Mountain Club, and is an avid Alpine skier, mountain biker, and certified master diver. Mr. Bragg resides in Centennial, Colorado. He has written the following books:

Accounting and Finance for Your Small Business
Accounting Best Practices
Accounting Control Best Practices
Accounting Policies and Procedures Manual
Billing and Collections Best Practices
Business Ratios and Formulas
The Controller's Function
Controller's Guide to Costing
Controller's Guide to Planning and Controlling Operations
Controller's Guide: Roles and Responsibilities for the New Controller
Controllership
Cost Accounting
Cost Reduction Analysis
Essentials of Payroll
Fast Close
Financial Analysis
GAAP Guide
GAAP Policies and Procedures Guide

GAAS Guide
Inventory Accounting
Inventory Best Practices
Investor Relations
Just-in-Time Accounting
Management Accounting Best Practices
Managing Explosive Corporate Growth
Mergers and Acquisitions
The New CFO Financial Leadership Manual
Outsourcing
Payroll Accounting
Payroll Best Practices
Revenue Recognition
Run the Rockies
Running a Public Company
Sales and Operations for Your Small Business
The Ultimate Accountants' Reference
The Vest Pocket Controller
Throughput Accounting
Treasury Management

FREE ONLINE RESOURCES BY STEVE BRAGG

Steve issues a free bimonthly accounting best practices newsletter and an accounting best practices podcast. You can sign up for both at www.stevebragg.com, or access the podcast through iTunes.

1 REVENUE RECOGNITION GENERAL PRINCIPLES AND SYSTEMS

OVERVIEW OF REVENUE RECOGNITION

The principles guiding recognition of revenues for financial reporting purposes are central to generally accepted accounting principles (GAAP) and International Financial Reporting Standards (IFRS) and in most instances are unambiguous and straightforward. In fact, the underlying principles have not changed in decades. However, as business transactions have become more complicated over time, GAAP and IFRS have expanded to include detailed rules for certain types of revenue recognition issues. Revenue recognition for GAAP is now aggregated under Topic 605 of the Accounting Standards Codification, while the same topic is somewhat more dispersed among IFRS source documents. This book summarizes these issues by topic and industry, covering such industries as motion pictures, software development, franchising, and real estate, while also addressing such cross-industry topics as situations when there is a right of return, or if collection is uncertain.

Each chapter begins with an overview of the topic, definitions of key terms, and a discussion of the key revenue recognition issues. If GAAP or IFRS mandates or recommends disclosure of revenue recognition information alongside the financial statements, then these disclosures are also noted, along with examples. Finally, a number of policies, procedures, and controls are covered that can support the systems needed to accumulate and report revenue transactions. These supporting systems are quite necessary, in light of the fraudulent reporting problems that are discussed later in this chapter.

REVENUE RECOGNITION GENERAL GUIDELINES

Revenue, whether from the sale of product or provision of services, is to be recognized only when it has been earned. According to the Statement of Financial Accounting Concepts No. 5 (CON 5), *Recognition and Measurement in Financial Statements of Business Enterprises,*

> ...*(a)n entity's revenue-earning activities involve delivering or producing goods, rendering services, or other activities that constitute its ongoing major or cen-*

> *tral operations, and revenues are considered to have been earned when the entity has substantially accomplished what it must do to be entitled to the benefits represented by the revenues.*

In other words, in order to be recognized, revenue must be realized or realizable, and it must have been earned.

CON 5 notes that "the two conditions (being realized or realizable, and being earned) are usually met by the time product or merchandise is delivered or services are rendered to customers, and revenues from manufacturing and selling activities and gains and losses from sales of other assets are commonly recognized at the time of sale (usually meaning delivery)." Moreover, "if services are rendered or rights to use assets extend continuously over time (for example, interest or rent), reliable measures based on contractual prices established in advance are commonly available, and revenues may be recognized as earned as time passes." In other words, for most traditional and familiar types of transactions, the point at which it is appropriate to recognize revenue will be quite clear.

The SEC's Revenue Recognition Criteria

The Securities and Exchange Commission (SEC), reflecting on the conceptual foundation for revenue recognition, observed in Staff Accounting Bulletin 104 (SAB 104), that

> *Revenue generally is realized or realizable and earned when **all** of the following criteria are met:*
> 1. *There is persuasive evidence that an arrangement exists,*
> 2. *Delivery has occurred or services have been rendered,*
> 3. *The seller's price to the buyer is fixed or determinable, and*
> 4. *Collectibility is reasonably assured.*

Note that while SEC rules and "unofficial" guidance are not necessarily to be deemed GAAP for nonpublic companies, to the extent that these provide insights into GAAP standards, they should always be viewed as relevant guidance and followed, absent other, contradictory rules established under GAAP. In the absence of any other source found in the GAAP rules, SEC pronouncements may represent the best thinking on the subject and are considered authoritative for all reporting entities.

With regard to the four criteria set forth above, consideration should be directed at the following discussion, which is drawn partially from SAB 104.

Persuasive Evidence of an Arrangement

First, regarding persuasive evidence of an arrangement, attention must be paid to the customary manner in which the reporting entity engages in revenue-producing transactions with its customers or clients. Since these transactions are negotiated between the buyer and seller and can have unique or unusual terms, there are (and can be) no absolute standards. Thus, for an enterprise that traditionally obtains appropriate documentation (purchase orders, etc.) from its customers before concluding sales to them, advance deliveries to customers, even if later ratified by receipt of the proper paperwork, would not be deemed a valid basis for revenue recognition at the time of delivery.

Example

The Minnetonka Motor Company has a new plastic engine available to ship to customers before the end of the current fiscal year. Wilson Trucks places an order for the new engine, and Minnetonka delivers the engine prior to the end of the year. Minnetonka's customary business practice is to require a signed sales agreement that must be signed by an authorized customer representative. Minnetonka issues the sales order, but the only person at Wilson authorized to sign the agreement is its president, who is on vacation. Wilson's purchasing manager has orally agreed to the contract and stated that it is highly likely that the president will sign the agreement upon his return from vacation.

Based on this scenario, the SEC does not believe that Minnetonka can recognize revenue in the current fiscal year, on the grounds that this arrangement has departed from Minnetonka's current business practice. In particular, the sales agreement is subject to a subsequent approval, which has not yet been obtained.

When evaluating purported revenue transactions, the substance of the transactions must always be considered, and not merely their form. It has become increasingly commonplace to "paper over" transactions in ways that can create the basis for inappropriate revenue recognition. For example, transactions that are actually consignment arrangements might be described as "sales" or as "conditional sales," but revenue recognition would not be appropriate until the consigned goods are later sold to a third-party purchaser.

Example

The Brass Fittings Company, maker of finely machined plumbing fittings, enters into an arrangement with Monaco Plumbing to deliver its products to Monaco on a consignment basis. The agreement specifically states that Monaco is the consignee, and that title to the products does not pass from Brass to Monaco until Monaco uses the fittings in its operations. Brass delivers product to Monaco and wants to recognize revenue at the time of shipment.

Based on this scenario, the SEC would not allow revenue recognition by Brass Fittings, on the grounds that products delivered to a consignee under a consignment arrangement are not sales and do not qualify for revenue recognition until a sale occurs. Revenue recognition is not appropriate, because Brass Fittings retains the risks and rewards of ownership, and title has not passed to Monaco.

Careful analysis of the rights and obligations of the parties and the risks borne by each at various stages of the transactions should reveal when and whether an actual sale has occurred and whether revenue recognition is warranted. The SEC believes that one or more of the following characteristics of a sale arrangement will preclude revenue recognition, *even if title to the product has passed to the buyer:*

1. The product is intended to be for demonstration purposes.
2. The seller is obligated to repurchase the product at specific prices, where the repayment prices are adjustable to cover the costs incurred by the buyer to purchase and hold the product.
3. The buyer can return the product and
    a. The buyer does not pay at the time of sale and is not obligated to do so on any specific dates; or
    b. The buyer's obligation to pay is excused until the buyer resells or uses the product; or
    c. The buyer will not have to pay if the product is damaged or destroyed; or
    d. The buyer has no economic substance except for that provided by the seller; or
    e. The seller has major obligations to assist the buyer in reselling the product.

Example

Scenario 1. The Guttering Candle Company, maker of beeswax candles, runs a special promotion during the slow first quarter of the year, where it refunds a portion of the original purchase price that is calculated based on the holding period of each buyer until such time as the buyer resells the candles to its customers.

Scenario 2. Guttering Candle pays interest costs on behalf of buyers under a third-party financing arrangement, until such time as they sell candles acquired from Guttering Candle.

Scenario 3. Guttering Candle provides below-market financing to buyers for the period beyond its customary 30-day payment terms and until the candles are resold.

Based on these scenarios, the SEC would not allow Guttering Candle to recognize revenue at the point of initial sale, because it is adjusting the purchase price to cover the holding costs of buyers.

In some countries, sellers commonly retain a form of title to goods delivered to customers until paid, so they can recover the goods in the event of a buyer default. Sellers are not entitled to direct the disposition of the goods and cannot rescind the transaction. In such a case, the SEC allows the seller to recognize revenue at the time of delivery. Only when the seller retains other rights normally held by the buyer of the goods will the SEC consider the transaction to be consignment, and not allow revenue recognition. The buyer must assume the risks of ownership in all cases if revenue is to be recognized.

Example

The Tidal Energy Company produces electrical turbines that are triggered by wave action. It enters into a formal agreement to sell ten of its most advanced turbines to the government of Vanuatu, located on an atoll in the Pacific Ocean. Tidal's sales manager also enters into a side agreement with the Energy Minister of Vanuatu, allowing for the return of all ten turbines within one year of installation if they do not provide the rated power levels.

Based on this scenario, the SEC would not allow Tidal to recognize revenue at the point of initial sale, on the grounds that the side agreement indicates that Tidal must continue to perform for one year before the revenue can be finalized. Also, if the side agreement was not properly documented and approved by Tidal's management, this is also a control breach that Tidal should recognize under the Sarbanes-Oxley Act.

Delivery Has Occurred or Services Rendered

With regard to whether delivery has occurred or services have been rendered, ownership and risk taking must have been transferred to the buyer if revenue is to be recognized by the seller. Thus, if the seller is holding goods for delivery to the buyer because the buyer's receiving dock workers are on strike and no deliveries are being accepted, revenue generally cannot be recognized in the reporting period, even if these delayed deliveries are made subsequent to period-end. (There are limited exceptions to this general principle, typically involving a written request from the buyer for delayed delivery under a "bill-and-hold" arrangement, having a valid business purpose.)

The SEC frowns upon bill-and-hold transactions. It will generally not allow revenue recognition in either of the following circumstances:

- When a company completes manufacturing of a product and segregates the inventory within its facility; or
- When a company ships products to a third-party storage facility while retaining title to the product and payment by the buyer will not occur until it is delivered to the buyer.

The SEC bases its opinion on the underlying concepts that revenue recognition does not occur until the customer takes title to the goods and assumes the risks and rewards of ownership. Consequently, the SEC uses all of the following criteria when determining whether revenue should be recognized:

1. Ownership risk must pass to the buyer;
2. The customer makes a (preferably) written commitment to buy the goods;
3. The buyer must request that the sale be on the bill-and-hold basis, and have a substantial business purpose for doing so;
4. There is a reasonable delivery schedule for the goods;
5. The seller has no remaining performance obligations;
6. The goods have been segregated, and cannot be used to fill other orders received by the seller; and
7. The product must be complete.

The SEC further points out that these criteria are not a checklist that will guarantee revenue recognition if a company can structure a transaction to meet all of the requirements; they are general criteria used to examine the intent of a transaction. In addition, the following factors should be considered in making the revenue recognition determination:

1. Whether the seller has modified its standard billing and credit terms for the buyer;
2. The seller's past pattern of using bill-and-hold transactions;
3. Whether the buyer has assumed the risk of loss if the market value of the goods declines;
4. Whether the seller's custodial risks of the goods purportedly sold are insurable and insured; and
5. That the business reasons for the bill-and-hold arrangement have not imposed a contingency on the buyer's commitment to accept the goods.

The SEC further states that delivery has generally not occurred unless the product has been delivered to either the customer or another site specified by the customer. If the customer specifies delivery to a staging site but a substantial portion of the sales price is not payable until delivery is ultimately made to the customer, then revenue recognition must be delayed until final delivery to the customer has been completed.

Delivery, as used here, implies more than simply the physical relocation of the goods to the buyer's place of business. Rather, it means that the goods have actually been accepted by the customer, which, depending on the terms of the relevant contract, could be conditioned on whether inspection, testing, and/or installation have been completed, and the buyer has committed to pay for the items purchased. For revenue recognition to be justified, substantial performance of the terms of delivery must have occurred, and if any terms remain uncompleted, there should be a basis grounded on historical experience to assume that these matters will be satisfactorily attended to.

The SEC holds that revenue should not be recognized until such time as any uncertainty about customer acceptance of goods or services has been eliminated. This requires an examination of customer acceptance provisions in the purchase agreement. For example, the agreement may allow the customer to test the product or require additional services subsequent to delivery, such as product installation. If these provisions exist, the SEC assumes that the customer specifically bargained for their inclusion in the agreement, which makes them substantive parts of the agreement. Consequently, revenue cannot be recognized until either the customer has accepted the goods or services, or the acceptance provisions have lapsed.

The SEC states that formal customer sign-off on a contractual customer acceptance provision is not always necessary. Instead, the seller can demonstrate that the criteria specified in the acceptance provisions are satisfied.

The SEC considers customer acceptance provisions to take one of four general forms, which are

1. *Acceptance for trial or evaluation purposes.* The customer agrees to accept the product strictly for evaluation purposes, so title remains with the seller. The customer may then actively affirm acceptance or do so simply through the passage of time; in either case, this is essentially a consignment arrangement where the seller should not recognize revenue until the customer confirms that it will purchase the product.

2. *Acceptance granting a right to return or exchange on the basis of subjective issues.* The customer has the right to return the product if dissatisfied with it. In this case, a company can recognize revenue at the initial point of sale, but only if it can reasonably estimate the amount of future returns and accrue for them. If the seller cannot make this estimate, then it must wait until the right of return has expired before recognizing revenue.

3. *Acceptance based on seller-specified objective criteria.* The customer has a right of return or replacement if the delivered product is defective or fails to meet its published specifications. If the seller has already demonstrated that the product meets its specifications and can reasonably estimate the amount of defective products, then

it can create a warranty reserve and recognize revenue at the point of sale. If the seller cannot prove that the product meets its published specifications, then it should defer revenue recognition until the specifications have been achieved.

4. *Acceptance based on customer-specified objective criteria.* The customer has created a specific set of acceptance criteria that the seller must meet before the customer will accept the delivery. This is best achieved with a formal sign-off document. Alternatively, the seller can demonstrate that the delivered product meets the customer's criteria (such as through preshipment testing). However, it may not be possible to conduct such testing prior to delivery, because performance may vary based on how the product works in combination with the customer's other systems. In this case, revenue recognition should be deferred until the product is actually installed and meets the stated criteria. Also, the seller must evaluate its ability to enforce a payment claim in the absence of a formal sign-off. If payment enforcement would be difficult, then revenue recognition should be deferred until formal customer sign-off.

This is perhaps the most subjective of the four forms of customer acceptance, so the SEC states that it will not object to a determination that is well reasoned on the basis of the guidance just described.

Example

The Dense Air Corporation manufacturers air compressors in a variety of standard models. The contract for sale of every standard model provides for customer acceptance of the compressors after receipt and testing by the customer. The contract states that customers are entitled to a full refund if the equipment does not perform as specified. Customers can indicate their acceptance by signing a form, or by the passage of 45 days, as noted in the acceptance provisions. Dense Air tests all of its compressors prior to shipment to ensure that they meet specifications.

Dense Air receives an order for its standard Nitrox compressor model from Maldives Diving. Dense Air has produced that model for five years and has no reason to believe that it will behave differently at Maldives than it does in the Dense Air facility. Based on the circumstances, Dense Air can reasonably and reliably estimate the amount of its warranty obligation, and so can recognize revenue upon delivery of the equipment, along with an appropriate liability for warranty obligations.

Example

The Dense Air Corporation receives a special order for its Nitrox compressor from Compact Boat Company, which needs to fit the compressor into an unusually small space on one of its boats. In addition to the usual customer acceptance provisions, Compact Boat can reject the compressor if it does not fit into the specified dimensions. Dense Air creates an installation space having the exact dimensions of those specified by Compact Boat, and verifies that the compressor both fits into this space and operates within the specifications.

Though the contract with Compact Boat contains a clause that includes customer-specific criteria, Dense Air demonstrates that the compressor meets the customer's objective criteria before it has shipped. Consequently, Dense Air can recognize revenue upon delivery of the equipment, along with an appropriate liability for warranty obligations.

Example

The Dense Air Corporation receives an order for its Nitrox compressor from Graphite Solutions, which plans to incorporate the compressor into a new filling station for its spun-graphite air tanks, which store compressed gases at extremely high pressure. Graphite may reject the compressor if it fails to meet the standard specifications, or cannot be integrated into the new filling station. Dense Air has no experience with this type of filling station, and cannot test it in advance to ensure compliance with Graphite's needs. However, the compressor meets all of Dense Air's standard performance criteria.

Because Dense Air cannot demonstrate that the compressor meets Graphite's criteria prior to shipment, it should wait until the compressor is successfully integrated into the filling station before recognizing revenue.

In some instances there are multiple "deliverables"; in such cases, revenue is not recognized for any given element if later deliverables are essential for the functionality of the already delivered element. In other situations, such as in various licensing arrangements, physical "delivery" may occur well before product usage by the buyer can take place (e.g., software for the future year's tax preparation delivered before the current year-end), and revenue is not to be recognized prior to the initial date of expected use by the buyer.

In the case of many service transactions, large up-front fees are often charged, nominally in recognition of the selling of a membership, the signing of a contract, or for enrolling the customer in a program. (An example is initiation fees to join a health club where the terms of membership also obligate the member to pay ongoing fees.) Unless the services provided to the customer at inception are substantial, the presumption is that the revenue received has not been earned, but rather must be deferred and recognized, usually ratably, over the period that substantive services are provided. Thus, initiation fees are amortized over the membership period.

According to the SEC, there are numerous situations where a customer must pay an up-front fee as part of a purchase transaction. For example, the fee may involve the conveyance of a license, or the delivery of a product or service. In many cases, the customer would not have paid the fee if the seller were not involved on a continuing basis with the provision of additional services. For example

- *Access fee.* A Web site that hosts a variety of databases charges a fee to its customers for unrestricted access to its data, which requires minimal additional cost by the Web site once the user has been given access to the system.
- *Activation fee.* A phone company mandates an activation fee when it sets up phone services for a new customer, as well as monthly usage fees.
- *Hosting fee.* A Web hosting company charges a fee for hosting a customer's Web site, where most of the cost is incurred during the initial installation.
- *Initiation fee.* A health club sells a membership to a customer, which includes an initiation fee and a continuing monthly fee.
- *Listing fee.* A Web site charges advertisers a fee to list their products on its Web site for a designated period of time, where there is a minimal cost associated with the advertisement during the period when it is posted.
- *Technology access fee.* The holder of intellectual property and research services requires its customers to pay a fee for access to its proprietary technology, as well as a periodic fee for its research services.

In all of the preceding examples, the SEC holds that revenue recognition of up-front fees should be deferred, unless the fees are in exchange for products or services that represent the completion of a separate earnings process. In essence, customers are really purchasing the ongoing rights, products, or services that the seller is providing through its continuing involvement under the sales arrangement. Thus, the SEC does not consider such activities as selling a membership or providing initial set-up services to be discrete earnings events.

There may be instance where the seller is incurring significant up-front costs, and so feels justified in recognizing revenue to the extent of those costs. However, because there is no separate deliverable associated with these costs (just an initial set-up), the SEC will usually object to such treatment. In most situations, the SEC believes that the up-front fee is coupled with the continuing performance obligation related to the services or products subsequently delivered to the customer; based on this judgment, the SEC believes that up-front fees should be recognized as revenue as the seller provides products or services over the period of performance. A reasonable form of such recognition is to recognize the revenue systematically over the period of performance.

In cases where the seller is providing a service and requires an up-front fee, the SEC prefers that the fee be accounted for as revenue on a straight-line basis; this recognition shall be either over the term of the arrangement or the expected period during which services are to be performed, whichever is longer. The only situation where revenue is not recognized on a straight-line basis is when revenue is earned or obligations are fulfilled in a different pattern.

Even in cases where the seller's obligations to the buyer are inconsequential or perfunctory, the SEC believes that the substance of these transactions indicates that the buyer is paying for a service that is delivered over a period of time, which therefore calls for revenue recognition over the period of performance.

Price Is Fixed or Determinable

The seller's price to the buyer is fixed or determinable when a customer does not have the unilateral right to terminate or cancel the contract and receive a cash refund. Depending on customary practice, extended return privileges might imply that this condition has not been met in given circumstances. Prices that are conditional on the occurrence of future events are not fixed or determinable from the perspective of revenue recognition.

In theory, until the refund rights have expired, or the specified future events have occurred, revenue should not be recognized. As a practical matter, however, assuming that the amount of refunds can be reliably estimated (based on past experience, industry data, etc.), revenues, net of expected refunds, can be recognized on a pro rata basis. Absent this ability to reliably estimate, however, revenue recognition is deferred.

A contract with a customer may contain a provision where cancellation privileges expire ratably over a stated contractual period. If so, the SEC believes that the sales price is also determinable ratably over the stated term. This view does not apply to short-term rights of return, such as a money-back guarantee within the first 30 days of ownership by the customer.

If a company sells a membership fee that can be cancelled by customers for a full refund at any time during the membership period, then the SEC holds that revenue recognition cannot occur until the end of the contractual period. The reason for this position is that there is uncertainty as to whether the fee is fixed or determinable at any point before the end of the period, since the customer has the right to unilaterally terminate the contract and receive a refund. In the meantime, cash received for such fees should be recorded in a liability account.

The SEC has indicated that it will *not* object to the recognition of refundable membership fees, net of estimated refunds, over the membership term, but only if *all* of the following criteria have been met:

- *Large pool of data.* The estimates of terminations and refunded revenues are made from a large pool of homogeneous items.
- *Reliable refund estimates can be made.* This is not the case if there are recurring and significant differences between actual and estimated termination experience (even if the impact of the variance on the amount of estimated refunds is not material to the financial statements), or if there are recurring variances that are material to either revenue or net income in quarterly or annual financial statements.

The SEC believes that an estimate, for purposes of meeting this criterion, is not reliable unless there is only a remote possibility that material adjustments to previously recognized revenue would be required. The SEC further presumes that reliable estimates cannot be made if termination and refund privileges exceed one year.

- *Sufficient historical basis.* A company should have a sufficient basis of historical information upon which to base its refund estimates, and it expects that this information is predictive of future events. Such estimates should take account of the following:
  - Historical experience by class of customer and service type
  - Trends in the historical information and the reasons for those trends
  - The impact of competing products or services
  - Changes in the ease with which customers can obtain refunds
- *Fixed membership fee.* The amount of the membership fee was fixed at the beginning of the agreement.

Only if *all* of these criteria are met will the SEC allow revenue recognition for the membership fee prior to the termination of customer refund rights. If revenue is recognized under these criteria, then a company should record the initial fees received from customers in two accounts:

- The amount of the fee representing estimated refunds is credited to a monetary liability account, such as "Fees refundable to customers."

- The amount of the fee representing unearned revenue is credited to a nonmonetary liability account, such as "Unearned revenues."
- When this accounting treatment is used, the company should disclose the following items with its financial statements:
  - The amount of unearned revenue
  - Refund obligations at the beginning of the period
  - Total cash received from customers
  - Revenue recognized in earnings
  - Total refunds paid
  - Other adjustments
  - Ending balances of unearned revenue and refund obligations

If a company recognizes refundable fee revenue ratably, then it should use a retrospective approach when adjusting for changes in estimated refunds. Under this method, unearned revenue and refund obligations are remeasured and adjusted at each balance sheet date, with the offsetting debit or credit being recorded as earned revenue.

A company does not have to recognize revenue ratably as allowed under the criteria in this section. The SEC will also allow the complete deferral of all related revenue until the refund period lapses, even if a company meets all of the criteria noted here. However, the company should disclose its recognition policy and apply it consistently for similar transactions.

Collectibility Is Reasonably Assured

The final factor, reasonable assurance of collectibility, implies that the accrual for bad debts (uncollectible accounts receivable) can be estimated with reasonable accuracy, both to accomplish proper periodic matching of revenue and expenses and to enable the presentation of receivables at net realizable value, as required under GAAP. An inability to accomplish this objective necessitates deferral of revenue recognition—generally until collection occurs, or at least until it becomes feasible to estimate the uncollectible portion with sufficient accuracy.

An extreme situation, calling for not merely accrual of losses from estimated uncollectible receivables, is to defer revenue recognition entirely until collectibility is assured (or actually achieved). The most conservative accounting alternative, first set forth in Accounting Research Bulletin No. 43 (ARB 43) and then again cited in CON 5, is to record revenue only as collected. It states "if collectibility of assets received for product, services, or other assets is doubtful, revenues and gains *may* be recognized on the basis of cash received" (emphasis added). The permissive language, which (it must be assumed) was deliberately selected in preference to a mandatory exhortation (e.g., "must"), suggests that even in such a situation, this hyperconservative departure from accrual accounting is not truly prescriptive but is a possible solution to a fact-specific set of circumstances.

The SEC mandates that, if a portion of a contract price is withheld or refundable until an outstanding service is delivered, then the revenue associated with that portion of the contract should not be recognized until the service has been completed.

Inconsequential Performance Obligations

The SEC holds that revenue may be recognized in its entirety if the seller's remaining obligation is inconsequential or perfunctory. This means that the seller should have substantially completed the terms specified in the sales arrangement in order for delivery or performance to have occurred. Any remaining incomplete actions can only be considered inconsequential if the failure to complete them would not result in the customer receiving a refund or rejecting the products or services. Further, the seller should have a history of completing the remaining tasks in a timely manner, and of being able to estimate all remaining costs associated with those activities. If revenue is recognized prior to the completion of any inconsequential items, then the estimated cost of those inconsequential items should be accrued when the revenue is recognized.

Given the ability to recognize revenue prior to the completion of inconsequential or perfunctory items, it is important to define these terms. In brief, a performance obligation is not inconsequential or perfunctory if it is essential to the functionality of the delivered products or services. Further, failure to complete them should result in the buyer receiving either a full or partial refund, or rejecting the delivered products or services. Also, it is possible that revenue recognition cannot occur if the company has a history of allowing refund or rejection rights in its prior contracts for these items, even if those terms are not present in the contract under consideration.

The SEC also considers the following factors as indicators that a remaining performance is substantive, rather than inconsequential or perfunctory:

- *Consistency.* The seller does not have a demonstrated history of completing the remaining tasks in a timely manner, nor of estimating their associated costs.
- *Cost.* The cost to extinguish the obligation is not insignificant in proportion to such items as the total revenue, gross profit, and operating income associated with the contract.
- *Duration.* The period before the remaining obligation will be extinguished is lengthy.

- *Payment timing.* Buyers issue payment of a portion of the sales price at approximately the same time that remaining performance is completed.
- *Requirements.* The skills or equipment needed to extinguish the obligation are specialized or not readily available in the marketplace.
- *Variability.* The cost or time needed to extinguish the obligation for similar contracts has historically been quite variable.

The SEC also mandates that a seller's determination of whether remaining obligations are inconsequential or perfunctory should be consistently applied. Thus, it is advisable to use a standard procedure and checklist for making this determination.

Conjoined Equipment and Installation

The SEC holds that, if the sale of equipment and related installation activities cannot be separated for revenue recognition purposes, then revenue recognition cannot take place until installation is complete. This situation arises when the equipment does not have value to the customer prior to installation, there is no evidence of fair value for the installation, or the buyer has a right of return when the installation is not considered probable.

Indicators that installation is essential to the functionality of an equipment sale are that installation services are not available from other suppliers, and that the installation involves significant changes to the equipment or building complex interfaces or connections.

However, installation is not essential to equipment functionality if the equipment is a standard product, installation does not significantly alter the equipment's capabilities, and other companies can also perform the installation.

Example

A/R Software Company owns CollectNow, which is a software package designed to assist the receivable collection staffs of its clients in their efforts to track outstanding receivables. It is installed on top of each client's accounting software, so that it can extract information from the receivables and customer master files. These interfaces are complex, and are usually individually created for each client. If a client owns an accounting package for which A/R has previously created interfaces, then the installation is much easier and more predictable.

A/R sells CollectNow to Pueblo Pottery, a figurine manufacturer. Pueblo uses the PottAlot accounting package, which is specific to the pottery industry, and for which it has not developed any interfaces. In this situation, CollectNow is useless to Pueblo Pottery until it is installed, and A/R must create several complex interfaces in order to make it function properly. In this situation the proper accounting treatment is to not recognize any revenue until the installation is complete and the CollectNow software is functional with Pueblo's software.

License Fee Revenue

In a situation where a company delivers and receives payment for intellectual property, the SEC holds that it cannot begin to recognize any revenue associated with the transaction until the beginning of the licensing period. At that point, the seller should recognize revenue in a manner consistent with the nature of the transaction and the earnings process.

Layaway Sales

In a situation where a retailer offers layaway privileges to its customers, the retailer retains the merchandise and collects a cash deposit from the customer; the customer does not receive the merchandise until the full price is paid, and the retailer can retain the deposit if the customer fails to pay the remainder of the amount due. In this scenario, the SEC states that the retailer should only recognize revenue under the layaway program when it has delivered the merchandise to the customer. Prior to that time, deposits should be recorded as a liability. The SEC would object to recognizing deposits as revenue, on the grounds that the retailer still owns the merchandise, has only received a deposit, and has no right to the remainder of the purchase price.

Defense of Intellectual Property

If a company has a patent on its intellectual property, and it licenses the property to customers, the company may represent to the customers that it will maintain and defend the patent. The SEC holds that it is not allowable to characterize this obligation as a deliverable to the customer, which might otherwise impact the timing of revenue recognition.

Estimates and Changes in Estimates

GAAP accounting requires that a company create a reserve for product returns in sales transactions where a right of return exists. Under GAAP, the following factors may impair a company's ability to make a reasonable estimate of product returns:

- *Demand changes.* Susceptibility of the product to such external factors as technological obsolescence or changes in demand.
- *No history.* Absence of historical experience with similar types of sales of similar products. This is a particularly common issue for

start-up companies and companies selling new or significantly modified products.

- *No homogeneity.* Absence of a large volume of relatively homogenous transactions.
- *Return duration.* Long periods in which a product may be returned.

In addition, the SEC has developed a list of factors that may preclude a company from developing a reliable estimate of product returns, which are

- *Channel stuffing.* Excessive levels of inventory in a distribution channel.
- *Competing products.* Newly introduced competing products having either superior technology or an increased level of expected market acceptance.
- *Distributor dominance.* A large proportion of the company's business, sales, and marketing with a particular distributor.
- *New Product.* A new product for which there is no historical return information.
- *Obsolescence.* New product introductions that will increase the amount of returns of current products.
- *Sales visibility.* Lack of visibility into the inventory levels in a distribution channel or the amount of sales to end-users.
- *Other.* Other factors affecting market demand and trends in that demand for the company's products.

If a sales transaction cannot meet all of the above conditions, a company cannot recognize any of the revenue associated with the transaction until either the conditions have been met or the return privilege has substantially expired, whichever occurs first. The SEC does not feel that creating a reserve based on the maximum possible amount of returns is an acceptable alternative method.

Contingent Rental Income

A lessor may enter into an agreement with a lessee under which the lessor is entitled to payments from the lessee that are contingent on subsequent business events. According the SEC, the lessor may not accrue the contingent revenue even if it will probably occur. Instead, such revenue can only be recognized when the underlying event actually occurs.

Example

Hempstead Properties leases retail office space to Stork, a purveyor of baby clothes. Under the terms of the one-year lease, Stork pays Hempstead $25,000 per month, plus one percent of its revenue that exceeds $15 million during the one-year term of the lease. Stork has consistently generated $18 million revenue from this store in the past, and will probably generate similar sales during the lease period, which would entitle Hempstead to an additional payment of $30,000. Stork typically generates the same amount of revenue in each month of the year.

Stork should reach the $15 million threshold sales level at the end of the tenth month of the lease, so Hempstead can recognize an additional $15,000 of revenue in both the eleventh and twelfth months of the lease.

Claims Processing and Billing Services

A common reimbursement clause in a contract to provide claims processing and billing services is that the service provider is entitled to some portion of collected amounts. The SEC holds that the service provider cannot accrue revenue for such services, but must instead wait until collection occurs before recognizing revenue.

Example

Zork Claims Processing provides claims processing services for health providers, whereby it prepares, submits, and collects on claims to third-party insurance companies. In exchange for these services, Zork receives 3% of the amount collected. Zork has considerable historical evidence that third-party insurance companies pay 82% of the billings it submits to them.

Zork must wait until it collects funds from the insurance companies before it can recognize any revenue, on the grounds that its revenue is not realized until the point of collection.

REVENUE RECOGNITION FRAUD

Though the basic principles of revenue recognition are uncomplicated, it is nonetheless true that a large fraction of financial reporting frauds have been the result of misapplications, often deliberate, of revenue recognition practices prescribed under GAAP. Apart from outright fraud (e.g., recording nonexistent transactions), there were several factors contributing to this unfortunate state of affairs.

First, business practices have continued to grow increasingly complex, involving, among other things, a marked shift from manufacturing to a services-based economy, where the proper timing for revenue recognition is often more difficult to ascertain. Second, there has been an undeniable increase in the willingness of managers, whose compensation packages are often directly linked to the company's stock price and reported earnings, to "stretch" accounting rules to facilitate earnings management. This has particularly been the case where GAAP requirements have been vague or complex. And third, it has been well documented that independent auditors have sometimes been willing to accommodate managements' wishes, particularly in the absence of specific rules under GAAP to support a denial of such requests. These actions have often had disastrous consequences.

Errors or deliberate distortions involving revenue recognition fall into two categories: situations in which revenue legitimately earned is reported in the incorrect fiscal (financial reporting) period, often referred to as "cutoff" errors, and situations in which revenue is recognized although never actually earned. Given the emphasis on periodic reporting (e.g., quarterly earnings announcements in the case of publicly held entities), even simple "cutoff" errors can have enormous impact, notwithstanding the fact that these should tend to offset over several periods. As a practical matter, all instances of improper revenue recognition are very serious, and these constitute a challenge to all accountants attempting to properly interpret and apply GAAP.

EVOLVING PROBLEMS IN REVENUE RECOGNITION

Certain problems currently found in the application of the general principles of revenue recognition, which can sometimes lead to fraudulent reporting, are discussed in the following paragraphs.

Financial Statement Presentation: Gross vs. Net

In general, it is well established that reporting on a "gross" basis is appropriate when the entity takes ownership of the goods being sold to its customers, with the risks and rewards of ownership accruing to it. For example, if the entity runs the risk of obsolescence or spoilage during the period it holds the merchandise, gross reporting would normally be appropriate. However, if the entity merely acts as an agent for the buyer or seller from whom it earns a commission, then "net" reporting would be more appropriate.

In recent years there have been increasing reports of enterprises that inflate revenues reported in their income statements by reporting transactions on a "gross" basis, notwithstanding that the entity's real economic role is as an agent for buyer and/or seller. This distortion became widespread in the case of Internet companies and other start-up businesses typically not reporting earnings, for which market valuations were heavily influenced by absolute levels of and trends in gross revenues. Reporting revenues "gross" rather than "net" often had an enormous impact on the perceived value of those enterprises.

The following factors should be considered when determining whether revenue is to be reported as the net retainage (hereinafter, "net") or the gross amount billed to a customer ("gross"). None of the indicators are presumptive or determinative, although the relative strength of each indicator is to be considered.

- Is the company the primary obligor in the arrangement; that is, is the company responsible for the fulfillment of the order, including the acceptability of the product or service to the customer? If the company, rather than a supplier, is responsible, that fact is a strong indicator that the company records revenue gross. Responsibility for arranging transportation for the product is not responsibility for fulfillment. If a supplier is responsible for fulfillment, including the acceptability to the customer, that fact indicates that the company recognizes only the net retainage.
- Does the company have general inventory risk? General inventory risk exists if a company takes title to a product before the product is ordered by a customer or will take title to the product if the customer returns it (provided that the customer has a right of return). In considering this indicator, arrangements with a supplier that reduce or mitigate the company's risk level are to be considered. Unmitigated general inventory risk is a strong indicator that the company recognizes revenue gross.
- Does the company have physical loss inventory risk? Physical loss inventory risk exists if the title to the product is transferred to the company at the shipping point and then transferred to the customer upon delivery. Physical loss inventory risk also exists if a company takes title to the product after the order is received but before the product is transferred to the shipper. While less persuasive than general inventory risk, this indicator provides some evidence that a company records revenue gross.
- Does the company establish the selling price? If a company establishes the selling price, that fact may indicate that the company recognizes revenue gross.
- Is the amount earned by the company fixed? If a company earns a fixed amount per transaction or if it earns a percentage of the selling price, that fact may indicate that the company reports revenue net.
- Does the company change the product or perform part of the service? If a company changes the product (beyond packaging) or performs part of the service ordered by the customer such that the selling price is greater as a result of the company's efforts, that fact is indicative that a company recognizes revenue gross. Marketing skills, market coverage, distribution system, and reputation are not to be evaluated in determining whether the company changes the product or performs part of the service.

- Does the company have multiple suppliers for the product or service ordered by the customer? If a company has the discretion to select the supplier, that fact may indicate that the company records revenue gross.
- Is the company involved in determining the nature, type, characteristics, or specifications of the product or service by the customer? If so, that fact may indicate that the company records revenue gross.
- Does the company have credit risk for the amount billed to the customer? Credit risk exists if a company must pay the supplier after the supplier performs, regardless of whether the customer has paid. If the company has credit risk, this fact provides weak evidence that the company records revenue gross. If the supplier assumes the credit risk, the company is to record revenue net.

The decision tree in Exhibit 1.1 shows the criteria that a company must pass before it can record revenue at the gross amount. All the criteria must be satisfied; otherwise, only the commission or broker fee associated with the sale can be recorded as revenue.

Exhibit 1.1: Decision tree for recording revenue at gross or net

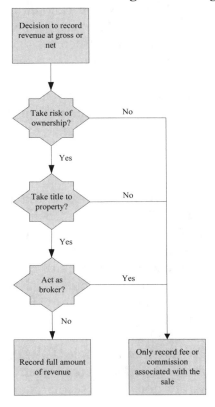

Barter Transactions

Barter transactions (nonmonetary exchanges) are not a problem, assuming that they represent the culmination of an earnings process. However, in recent years there have been reports of transactions that appear to have been concocted merely to create the illusion of revenue-generating activities. Examples include advertising swaps engaged in by some entities, most commonly "dot-com" enterprises, and the excess capacity swaps of fiber-optic communications concerns under "indefeasible right to use" agreements. Both these and many other situations involved immediate recognition of revenues coupled with deferred recognition of costs, and typically, in aggregate, were equal exchanges not providing profits to either party. Furthermore, these examples do not represent culminations of the normal earnings process (e.g., fiber-optic networks were built in order to sell communications services to end users, not for the purpose of swapping capacity with other similar operations).

In hindsight, most observers can see why these and many other aggressive reporting practices deviated from established or implied GAAP; although there are still some who insist that because GAAP failed to explicitly address these precise scenarios, the accounting for the transactions was open to interpretation. Since GAAP cannot possibly hope to address all the various innovative transaction structures that exist and will be invented, it is necessary to apply basic principles and reason by analogy to newly emerging circumstances. Of great importance to financial statement preparers (and internal and external auditors) are obtaining a thorough understanding of the nature and normal operations of the business enterprise being reported upon, application of "substance over form" reasoning, and the goal of faithfully representing the economics of transactions.

Channel Stuffing

Many difficult issues of revenue recognition involve practices that may or may not involve GAAP departures, depending on the facts and circumstances. Channel stuffing is a prime example of this issue, where sales are actually made prior to the period-end cutoff but are stimulated by "side agreements," such as a promise to customers of extended return privileges or more liberal credit terms. In such circumstances, there might be a greater likelihood that a substantial portion of these sales may be subsequently nullified, as unrealistically large orders inevitably lead to later large returns made for full credit.

For purposes of financial reporting under GAAP, valuation allowances should be established for expected sales returns and allowances. (In practice, however, this is rarely done because the amounts involved are immaterial, unlike the amounts of the more familiar allowances for uncollectible accounts.) The use of valuation accounts for anticipated returns and allowances is dictated by both the matching concept (recording returns and allowances in the same fiscal period in which the revenue is recognized) as well as by the requirement to present accounts receivable at net realizable value. When the potential product returns are not subject to reasonable estimation (as when a sales promotion effort of the type just described is first being attempted by the reporting entity) but could be material, it might not be permissible to recognize revenues at all, pending subsequent developments. Furthermore, from the SEC's perspective, factors such as the following could require deferral of revenues at the time goods are shipped to customers, pending resolution of material uncertainties:

1. Significant levels of product inventory in the distribution channel
2. Lack of "visibility" into, or the inability to determine or observe, the levels of inventory in a distribution channel and the current level of sales to end users
3. Expected introductions of new products that may result in the technological obsolescence of, and larger than expected returns of, current products
4. The significance of a particular distributor to the company's (or a reporting segment of the company's) business, sales, and marketing
5. The newness of a product
6. The introduction of competitors' products with superior technology or greater expected market acceptance could affect market demand and changing trends in that demand for an entity's products.

Mischaracterization of Extraordinary or Unusual Transactions as Components of Gross Revenue

Not all revenue recognition errors and frauds involve questions of when or if revenue should be recognized. In some instances, classification in the income statement is of greater concern. While matters in this group often do not result in a distortion of net results of operations, they can seriously distort important indicators of performance trends. When this occurs, it most often involves reporting unusual or infrequent gains on sales of segments or specific assets as revenue from product or service transactions. A variation on this involves reporting unusual gains as offsets to one or more categories of operating expenses, similarly distorting key financial ratios and other indicators, again without necessarily invalidating the net income measure.

Mischaracterizing Transactions as Involving "Arm's-Length" Third Parties, Thus Justifying Unwarranted Gain Recognition

Transfers of inventory or other assets to a related entity typically defers gain or income recognition until subsequent transfer to an "arm's-length" party. In some cases, sales have been disguised as being to unrelated entities with gain being recognized, when in fact the "buyer" was a nominee of the seller, or the financing was provided or guaranteed by the seller, or the "buyer" was a "variable interest entity" that failed to meet the complex requirements under GAAP required for gain recognition. Depending on the facts of the situation, this can result in gains being improperly recognized or the gross amount of the transaction being improperly recognized in the seller/transferor's financial statements.

Selling Undervalued Assets to Generate Reportable Gains

This issue again ranges from deliberate but real economic transactions that have as a goal the inflation of reportable revenues or gains, to misrepresented events having no economic substance but the same objective. Among the former is the deliberate invasion of low-cost last-in, first-out (LIFO) inventory "layers," which boosts gross margins and net profits for the period, albeit at the cost of having to later replenish inventories with higher-cost goods. To the extent that this depletion of lower-cost inventory really occurs, there is no GAAP alternative to reflecting these excess profits currently, although the threat of full disclosure may prove to be somewhat of a deterrent.

Regarding the latter category, in some instances the ability to generate gains could indicate that errors occurred in recording a previous transaction. Thus, large gains flowing from the sale of assets recently acquired in a purchase business combination transaction could well mean the purchase price allocation process was flawed. If this is true, a reallocation of purchase price would be called for, and some or all of the apparent gains would be eliminated.

Related to the foregoing is the strategy of retiring outstanding debt in order to generate reportable gains. In periods of higher-than-historical interest rates, lenders will agree to early extinguishment of outstanding obligations at a discount, hence creating gains for the borrower, albeit replacement debt at current yields will result in higher interest costs over future years. To the extent the debt is really retired, however, this is a real economic event, and the consequent gain is reported in current earnings under GAAP.

Deliberate Misstatement of Percentage of Completion on Long-Term Construction Contracts

Profits on certain long-term construction-type contracts are to be recognized ratably over the period of construction. An obvious and often easy way to distort periodic results of operations is to deliberately over- or understate the degree to which one or more discrete projects has been completed as of period-end. This, coupled with the difficulty and importance of estimating remaining costs to be incurred to complete each project, makes profit recognition under this required method of accounting challenging to verify.

DISCLOSURES

According to the SEC, companies are required to disclose their revenue recognition policies. This should include disclosure of

- The revenue recognition policy for each material type of transaction
- If the company enters into multiple-element sales arrangements (e.g., bundling of related products and/or services), the method of accounting for each element and the method used to determine each element and value it
- Material changes in estimates of returns (e.g., changing the percentage of sales used to establish the allowance)

Sample disclosures are

1. The company sells maintenance agreements along with its home air conditioning units. Maintenance revenue is recognized ratably over the term specified within each agreement, which can range from 12 to 60 months. In cases where maintenance agreements are offered to customers at a discount, the company assumes that the discounts really apply to the complete package of air conditioning products and related maintenance agreements, and so recalculates the discount as a percentage of the entire package. This results in approximately 65% of the discounts being assigned to product sales and the remaining 35% to maintenance sales. The adjusted maintenance revenues are then recognized ratably over the term specified within each agreement. As of the balance sheet date, $1,389,000 of maintenance revenues had not been recognized.

2. The company sells electrical appliance monitoring devices to large industrial manufacturers. It charges a nominal amount for each unit

sold and takes 5% of the electricity savings generated from the use of each unit for the first three years after which each unit is installed, up to a maximum of $5,000 per quarter. Given the uncertainty of the savings to be generated from electricity cost savings, the company does not feel that it can reasonably recognize any revenue until after cost savings have been determined at the end of each quarter. Also, since cost savings tend to be disputed by recipients, making cash receipts problematic, management has elected to further delay revenue recognition until after cash has been received from each customer.

In addition, SEC Regulation S-X requires that each of the following four categories of revenue (and the related costs), if applicable, be stated separately on the face of the income statement:

1. Sales of tangible products (net of discounts, returns, and allowances)
2. Income from rentals
3. Revenue from services
4. Other revenues

Bill-and-hold transactions are generally frowned upon, given the risk of abuse by companies that can use this technique to inflate their revenues. Consequently, if any bill-and-hold transactions are used, it is best to disclose this information, clearly stating that the company follows all GAAP requirements for such transactions, and also noting the dollar amount and percentage of revenues involved, and any change in the level of bill-and-hold revenue from the preceding year. An example follows.

> During the past year, the company sold $172,000 of stoves to its restaurant customers under "bill-and-hold" transactions. Under these arrangements, restaurant owners asked the company to retain stoves in its warehouse facilities until new restaurants had been built to accommodate them. These customers acknowledged in writing that they had ordered the inventory, that the company was storing the stoves on their behalf, that they had taken on all risks of ownership, and that the stoves would be delivered in no more than three months. Total bill-and-hold transactions were $15,000 lower than the $187,000 in similar transactions that occurred in the preceding year. In both years, bill-and-hold transactions comprised 14% of total company revenues.

Barter transactions should be recognized at the fair market value of the assets received in an exchange. The nature of any such transactions should be disclosed, as well as the approximate value of the transactions and how they are recorded in the financial statements. An example follows.

The company provides aerial traffic reports to a number of radio stations, for which they give airtime to the company. The company then obtains advertising to run on these free minutes, from which it collects the proceeds. The company recognizes revenue from these barter transactions only after advertisements have been obtained and have been run on the participating radio stations. No asset is recorded on the company balance sheet when airtime is received from radio stations, since there is still significant uncertainty that the company will be able to convert the airtime into paid advertisements. In 2010, the revenue recognized from these transactions was $1,745,000.

Shipments made to a distributor on consignment are not truly sales until sold by the distributor. The exact method of revenue recognition should be clearly disclosed, so readers can be sure that revenue is not recognized too soon in the sales process. Also, inventory may be shipped to a company by its customers on a consignment basis, to be included in custom products that are then sold back to the customers. Only the value added to these custom products should be recognized as revenue. The following footnotes show proper disclosure of these situations:

1. The company ships its eyewear products to a number of distributors, having no direct sales function of its own. All shipments to distributors continue to be recorded as inventory by the company until notification of shipment is received from distributors. In selected cases where there has been a problematic payment history by distributors, the company does not record revenue until cash has been received.

2. The company produces custom rockets for its payload launch customers. Several customers prefer to supply rocket engines to be incorporated into the company's rockets. Accordingly, these engines are recorded as consignment inventory when received and assigned a zero cost. When the completed rockets are shipped to customers, the price of the consigned engines is not included in the amount billed, thereby reducing the total revenue recognized by the company.

There is no specific GAAP requirement that a company state its policy regarding the use of an allowance for sales returns. However, if a reserve has been created, then a footnote should detail how the amount of the reserve was derived. An example follows.

The company recorded an allowance for sales returns of $148,000. This amount is based on a historical average rate of return of 12% of the company's subscription magazine business.

If a company has revenues from individual customers that amount to at least 10% of total revenues, then one must report the amount of revenues from each of these customers as well as the name of the business segment with which these customers are doing business. An example follows.

> The company does a significant amount of its total business with two customers. One customer, comprising 15% of total revenues for the entire company, also comprises 52% of the revenues of the appliances segment. The second customer, comprising 28% of total revenues for the entire company, also comprises 63% of the revenues of the government segment.

If sales are concentrated in foreign locations where there are risks of sales reductions due to political issues, then the extent of these sales and the types of risks should be disclosed. An example follows.

> The company sells 55% of its customer relationship management software through a distributor in Iran. Given the large proportion of company sales attributable to this supplier, any unrest in the region, such as wars, terrorist activity, or an enforced shutdown in business activities by the Iranian government, would have a material impact on the company's financial results.

REVENUE RECOGNITION POLICIES AND PROCEDURES

The following policies can be used to maintain a proper level of control over a company's timely and consistent application of revenue recognition rules:

- *Preliminary revenue summaries shall be issued no later than one day following the close of an accounting period.* This policy is designed to prevent the accounting staff from artificially keeping the books open past the end of the reporting period, since it must commit to a specific revenue figure within a day of closing.
- *Extended rights of return shall not be allowed.* This policy limits the ability of the sales staff to engage in "channel stuffing," since it cannot offer special rights of return to customers in exchange for early sales. The policy keeps a company from gyrating between large swings in sales caused by channel stuffing.
- *Special sale discounts shall not be allowed without senior management approval.* This policy prevents large bursts in sales caused by special price discounts that can stuff a company's distribution channels, causing rapid sales declines in subsequent periods.
- *The company shall not use bill-and-hold transactions.* Though bill-and-hold transactions are allowable under clearly defined and closely restricted circumstances, they are subject to abuse and so should generally be avoided. This policy ensures that bill-and-hold transactions would require board approval before being used.

- *Estimated profits on service contracts shall be reviewed monthly.* This policy ensures that estimated losses on service contracts are identified and recognized promptly, rather than being delayed until the contracts are closed.
- *The company shall not engage in barter transactions whose sole purpose is the creation of revenue.* This policy informs the accounting staff that it is unacceptable to create barter swap transactions whose sole purpose is to create additional revenue without the presence of any economic reason for the transaction.
- *All expenses associated with barter transactions shall be recognized in the same proportions as related revenues.* This policy is designed to keep expenses associated with barter swap transactions from being significantly delayed while revenues are recognized up front. The policy will keep profits from being incorrectly recorded in advance.

Shipping Procedure

A key element of the revenue recognition process is consistent use of a procedure for processing shipments to customers, since this is the source of documents later used by the billing department to create invoices. The basic shipment processing procedure is as follows:

1. Access the daily schedule of shipments in the computer system and print the report.
2. Verify that all finished goods listed on the daily schedule are on hand and available for shipment.
3. If the required quantities are not available, contact the customer service staff to ascertain customer wishes regarding partial orders, or contact the production scheduling staff to ensure that the production department will complete the missing products as soon as possible.
4. Mark all other items on the daily schedule as being ready for delivery.
5. Using the daily schedule, remove all targeted items from the warehouse bins and relocate them to the shipping area.
6. Contact freight carriers regarding scheduled pickup times.
7. Prepare bills of lading and packing slips for all shipments.
8. Load shipments on trucks for delivery.
9. Complete the shipping log.
10. Send copies of the bills of lading and packing slips to the accounting department by interoffice mail. Include a copy of the day's shipping log, which should match all other documentation sent.

11. Access the computer system and enter the customer, ship date, part number, and quantity shipped for each shipment sent out that day.

Billing Procedure

Once all shipping information has been compiled by the accounting department, its billing staff must convert this information into an invoice that is used to recognize revenue. The billing procedure is as follows:

1. Receive the daily packet of shipping information from the warehouse manager. The paperwork should include a handwritten shipping log as well as two copies of the bills of lading. Print the customer order from the computer system. Separate these documents into different piles.

2. Verify that there is a bill of lading for every order listed on the shipping log and also that *all* bills of lading are listed on the log. Then put the bills of lading in order, first by customer name and then by order number (if there is more than one order per customer), and match the order forms to them.

3. Check the "carrier" column on the shipping log. There is no shipping charge if "customer pickup" is noted. Otherwise, if a carrier name is listed, calculate a freight rate based on the standard freight rate schedule. Note the amount of the freight charge on the order form.

4. Go to the invoicing module in the accounting software and access the invoicing screen. Enter the customer name and verify that the Bill To name in the system is correct. If not, change it to match the name listed on the order. Then enter the part number, quantity, and price listed on the order form. Add the freight rate to the bottom of the invoice. Also verify that the sales tax code is correct. Save the invoice record and repeat until all invoices have been entered.

5. Verify that the invoice form is correctly positioned in the printer. Run a test invoice if necessary to ensure that the form is properly aligned. Then print the daily invoice batch.

6. Burst all printed invoices, with the pink copies going to the alphabetical filing bin, the white copies going to customers, and the goldenrod copies going to the numerical filing bin.

7. Stuff the white invoice copies into envelopes and mail them to customers. If the system generates an electronic invoice, e-mail it to the customer.

8. Attach the pink invoice copies to the bills of lading, packing slip, and customer orders, and file them by customer name. File the goldenrod copies in numerical order.

Matching Billing to Shipping Log Procedure

Though the two preceding processes form the foundation of a revenue recognition system, it is also possible that various failings in the billing process will result in the underrecognition of revenue that is caused by shipments that are never billed. The following procedure is designed to detect these problems by comparing billing information to the shipping log:

1. Go to the warehouse and make a copy of the shipping log for the previous week. Alternatively (if available), access this information online through the receiving system and print out the shipping log.
2. Match the shipments listed on the shipping log to invoices issued during the same period. Note all exceptions in the shipping log for missing billings. Also, note on invoices any incorrect quantities that were billed, as well as "leftover" invoices for which there is no shipping record.
3. Using the list of shipments for which there are no corresponding invoices, go to the shipping department and obtain bills of lading for the unbilled shipments. If these are not available, determine which freight carrier shipped the items and obtain shipping traces on them. Then create invoices, mail a copy to the customer, and attach proof of delivery to the company's copy of the invoice. File the company's copy in the accounting files.
4. Using the list of invoices for which no corresponding shipment is recorded in the shipping log, go back to the company's copy of these invoices and see if there is any bill of lading or other proof of delivery attached to the invoice. If not, call the shipping department to verify that no such documentation exists there. If not, issue a credit to eliminate these invoices.
5. Using the list of invoices for which the quantity of product billed is different from the quantity shipped, go back to the company's copy of the invoice and check the attached bill of lading to determine the actual quantity shipped. If the quantity is different, verify this with the shipping department and then either issue a credit (if the quantity billed was too high) or an additional invoice (if the quantity billed was too low).

Pricing Review Procedure

It is also possible (if not likely) that some invoices will contain pricing errors, which will result in improper revenue recognition. The following procedure is designed to detect these errors:

1. Go to the accounting software and access the invoice register for the past month.
2. Convert the invoice register to an Excel file. Open the Excel file and sort the invoice list by dollar order. Delete all invoices from the list that do not have a credit balance.
3. Search the description field for each credit for wording regarding corrections of pricing errors. Retain these records and delete all others. Print the spreadsheet.
4. Transfer the following information to a separate spreadsheet report: credit number, credit amount, customer name, correct price, actual price charged, the quantity of product to which the correction applies, the grand total pricing error, and the initials of the customer service person who processed the credit.
5. Go to the customer service person who processed the credit and determine the cause of the pricing error. Include this information on the spreadsheet.
6. Print the spreadsheet and distribute it to the sales manager, controller, and chief operating officer.
7. Enter the total number of pricing errors and the total dollar error in the monthly corporate statistics report.

Bill-and-Hold Procedure

A common tool for reporting excessively high revenue levels is to bill customers for shipments that the company has not yet shipped, ostensibly because the customer has requested that the goods be kept in storage at the company's location. However, some of these "bill-and-hold" transactions are valid but present invoicing challenges because there is no product shipment to trigger a billing. The following procedure can be used to ensure that revenue is properly recognized:

1. Access the warehouse database on a specific recurring date and call up the report listing all bill-and-hold items currently in stock. Take the report to the warehouse and verify that all items listed on the report match what is in stock, and also trace all items in stock back to the report. Investigate any variances.
2. If the invoice number associated with each bill-and-hold item is not already listed in the report, retrieve this information from the file containing the last period's bill-and-hold transactions. Compare this information to the validated warehouse report and note any items that have not yet been billed.
3. For all bill-and-hold items not yet billed, print the Acknowledgment of Bill-and-Hold Transaction form (as shown in Exhibit 1.2)

and fax it to the authorized customer representative, with a request that it be signed and sent back.

4. Once the signed form has been received, verify that all signature spots have been signed. Then attach a copy of the customer's purchase order to the form, copy both, and send them to the billing staff for invoicing. Put the originals in a pending file.

5. Once the accounting staff creates the invoice, it will return an invoice copy. Attach this copy to the signed form and customer purchase order, staple them together, and file them by customer name.

6. When bill-and-hold items are eventually shipped to the customer, the warehouse staff removes them from the inventory database and sends the bill of lading to the accounting person handling the bill-and-hold transactions. This person removes the transaction's previously filed invoice packet from the files, attaches to it the bill of lading, and forwards the complete package to the billings staff, which then files the packet in the completed invoices file.

Exhibit 1.2: Acknowledgment of bill-and-hold transaction form

Acknowledgment of
Bill-and-Hold Transaction

Customer Name: _____

This document indicates your acknowledgment that a bill-and-hold transaction exists in regard to purchase order number _____, which you ordered from [company name]. Please indicate your acknowledgment of this transaction by initialing next to each of the following statements and signing at the bottom of the page. If you disagree with any of the statements, please indicate your concerns at the bottom of the page. Thank you!

_____　I agree that I ordered the items noted in the purchase order.
(initial)

_____　I agree that [company name] is storing the items noted in the pur-
(initial)　chase order on my behalf.

_____　I acknowledge that I have taken on all risks of ownership related to
(initial)　this purchase order.

_____　I agree that I requested the bill-and-hold transaction, and my reason
(initial)　for doing so is as follows:

_____

_____

_____　I agree that all performance issues related to this purchase order were
(initial)　completed no later than _____.

_____　I agree that the held goods will be delivered to me no later than ____
(initial)

_____

I disagree with some or all of the statements on this page. My concerns are as follows:

_____

_____

_____	_____
Signature	Date
_____	_____
Name (Please Print)	Title

REVENUE RECOGNITION CONTROLS

The following controls can be used to spot transactional errors or attempts to alter the reported level of revenue for the standard revenue recognition systems:

- **Investigate all journal entries increasing the size of revenue.** Any time a journal entry is used to increase a sales account, this should be a "red flag" indicating the potential presence of revenues that were not created through a normal sales journal transaction. These transactions can be legitimate cases of incremental revenue recognition associated with prepaid services, but can also be barter swap transactions or fake transactions whose sole purpose is to increase revenues.

  It is especially important to review all sales transactions where the offsetting debit to the sales credit is *not* accounts receivable or cash. This is a prime indicator of unusual transactions that may not really qualify as sales. For example, a gain on an asset sale or an extraordinary gain may be incorrectly credited to a sales account that would mislead the reader of a company's financial statements that its operating revenues have increased.

- **Compare the shipping log and shipping documents to invoices issued at period-end.** This control is designed to spot billings on transactions not completed until after the reporting period closed. An invoice dated within a reporting period whose associated shipping documentation shows the transaction as having occurred later is clear evidence of improper revenue reporting. If invoices are based on services instead of goods provided, then invoices can be matched to service reports or time sheets instead.

- **Issue financial statements within one day of the period-end.** By eliminating the gap between the end of the reporting period and the issuance of financial statements, it is impossible for anyone to create additional invoices for goods shipping subsequent to the period-end, thereby automatically eliminating any cutoff problems.

- **Compare customer-requested delivery dates to actual shipment dates.** If customer order information is loaded into the accounting computer system, run a comparison of the dates on which customers have requested delivery to the dates on which orders were actually shipped. If there is an ongoing tendency to make shipments substantially early, there may be a problem with trying to create revenue by making early shipments. Of particular interest is when there is a surge of early shipments in months when revenues would otherwise have been low, indicating a clear intention to increase revenues by avoiding customer-mandated shipment dates. It may be possible to program the computer system to not allow the recording of deliveries if the entered delivery date is prior to the customer-requested delivery date, thereby effectively blocking early revenue recognition.

- **Compare invoice dates to the recurring revenue database.** In cases where a company obtains a recurring revenue stream by billing customers periodically for maintenance or subscription services, there can be a temptation to create early billings in order to record revenue somewhat sooner. For example, a billing on a 12-month subscription could be issued after 11 months, thereby accelerating revenue recognition by one month. This issue can be spotted by comparing the total of recurring billings in a month to the total amount of recurring revenue for that period as compiled from the corporate database of customers with recurring revenue. Alternatively, compare the recurring billing dates for a small sample of customers to the dates on which invoices were actually issued.

- **Identify shipments of product samples in the shipping log.** A product that is shipped with no intention of being billed is probably a product sample being sent to a prospective customer, marketing agency, and so on. These should be noted as product samples in the shipping log, and the internal audit staff should verify that each of them was properly authorized, preferably with a signed document.

- **Verify that a signed Acknowledgment of Bill-and-Hold Transaction has been received for every related transaction.** If a company uses bill-and-hold transactions, then this control is absolutely mandatory. By ensuring that customers have agreed in advance to be billed for items to be kept in the company's warehouse, one can be assured of being in compliance with the strict GAAP and IFRS rules applying to these transactions. Also, a continual verification of this paperwork (shown earlier in Exhibit 1.2) will keep managers from incorrectly inflating revenues by issuing false bill-and-hold transactions.

- **Confirm signed Acknowledgment of Bill-and-Hold Transactions with customers.** If a company begins to match bill-and-hold acknowledgment letters to invoices issued to customers (see last control), the logical reaction of any person who wants to fraudulently continue issuing bill-and-hold invoices is to create dummy acknowledgments. Consequently, it is useful to contact the persons who allegedly signed the acknowledgments to verify that they actually did so.

- **Do not accept any product returns without an authorization number.** Customers will sometimes try to return products if there is no justification required, thereby clearing out their inventories at the expense of the company. This can be avoided by requiring a return authorization number, which must be provided by the company in advance and prominently noted on any returned goods. If the number is not shown, the receiving department is required to reject the shipment.

- **Compare related company addresses and names to customer list.** Compare the list of company subsidiaries to the customer list to determine if any intercompany sales have occurred and whether these transactions have all been appropriately backed out of the financial statements. Since employees at one subsidiary may conceal this relationship by using a false company name or address, verify the same information at all the other subsidiaries by matching subsidiary names and addresses to their supplier lists, since it is possible that the receiving companies are *not* trying to hide the intercompany sales information.

- **Require a written business case for all barter transactions.** Require the creation of a business case detailing why a barter transaction is required and what type of accounting should be used for it. The case should be approved by a senior-level manager before any associated entry is made in the general ledger. The case should be attached to the associated journal entry and filed. This approach makes it less likely that sham barter swap transactions will be created.

- **Verify that cash-back payments to customers are charged to sales.** Compare the customer list to the cash disbursements register to highlight all cash payments made to customers. Investigate each one and verify that the revenue account was debited in those instances where cash-back payments were made. This should not apply to the return of overpayments made by customers to the company.

- **Create a revenue accounting procedure to specify the treatment of gross or net transactions.** When a company deals with both gross and net revenue transactions on a regular basis, there should be a procedure that clearly defines for the accounting staff the situations under which revenues shall be treated on a gross or net basis. This reduces the need for internal audit reviews (see next control) to detect revenue accounting problems after the fact.

- **Review the revenue accounting for potential pass-through transactions**. In situations where there is either an extremely high cost of goods sold (indicating a possible pass-through transaction) or where there is no clear evidence of the company's acting as principal, taking title to goods, or accepting risk of ownership, the internal audit staff should review the appropriateness of the transaction.

- **Trace commission payments back to underlying sale transactions.** Keep a list of all business partners who pay the company commissions, and run a periodic search on all payments made by them to the company. The internal audit staff can then trace these payments back to the underlying sales made by the company and verify that they were recorded at net, rather than at gross.

The controls noted here are not comprehensive; additional controls are listed in subsequent chapters that apply to more detailed revenue recognition scenarios.

2 REVENUE RECOGNITION UNDER INTERNATIONAL FINANCIAL REPORTING STANDARDS

OVERVIEW

International accounting standards (IAS) do not quite enter into the level of detailed restrictions and rules so common in generally accepted accounting principles (GAAP). Instead, they set general guidelines, which allow users some interpretational leeway. Consequently, a great deal of territory will be covered within this chapter, which comprises the sum total of all IAS that has been issued to date on this topic. The primary sources of information for revenue recognition are IAS 11, *Construction Contracts*, IAS 18, *Revenue*, and IAS 41, *Agriculture*.

The revenue standards in this chapter apply to revenue arising from the following transactions and events:

- **Agricultural produce.** The harvested product of an entity's biological assets.
- **Goods.** Those goods produced by the entity for the purpose of sale. Also, goods purchased for resale, such as toys purchased by a children's products retailer. This also applies to land and property acquired for resale.
- **Services.** Performance by an entity of contractually mandated tasks over time.
- **Interest.** Charges for the use of cash owned by the entity.
- **Royalties.** Charges for the use of such entity assets as patents, trademarks, and copyrights.
- **Dividends.** Profit distributions to equity investment holders.

DEFINITIONS OF TERMS

Construction contract. A contract specifically intended for the construction of an asset or closely interrelated combination of assets.

Cost plus contract. A construction contract where the contractor is reimbursed for defined costs, plus either a percentage of these costs or a fixed fee.

Fair value. The amount for which an asset could be exchanged, or a liability settled, between knowledgeable, willing parties in an arm's-length transaction.

Fixed price contract. A construction contract where the contractor accepts a fixed contract price or a fixed rate per unit of output, which may be subject to cost escalation clauses.

Revenue. Income that arises through the ordinary activities of an entity, and is referred to as sales, fees, interest, dividends, and royalties. It is the gross inflow of economic benefits during the period arising in the course of the ordinary activities of an entity when those inflows result in increases in equity, other than increases relating to contributions from equity participants.

REVENUE MEASUREMENT FOR GOODS

Fair Value Measurement

Revenue is measured at the fair value of the consideration received, taking into account the amount of any trade discounts and volume rebates accepted by the entity. When paid in cash, the amount of revenue recognized shall be the amount of cash received or receivable.

Deferred Payments

In the event of a deferred cash payment, the fair value of the consideration received may be reduced. When a delayed payment effectively constitutes a financing transaction, revenue shall be recognized as the discounted cash flow of the transaction, using an imputed interest rate that is the more clearly determinable of either (1) the prevailing interest rate for a similar transaction by an entity with a similar credit rating; or (2) a rate of interest that discounts the transaction to the current cash price of the underlying goods or services.

If a transaction is discounted for revenue recognition purposes, then the difference between the fair value and face value of the consideration paid is recorded as interest revenue.

Example

Somnolent Sofas is offering a year-end deal for its luxury leather sofas, under which customers can either pay €2,000 in cash or a zero down payment with 24 monthly payments of €100 each, totaling €2,400. Since there is a difference of €400 between the cash price and the extended terms, the zero-down-payment deal is essentially comprised of separate financing and sale transactions. For any sale under the zero-down-payment plan, Somnolent should record a sale of €2,000, which is the amount of consideration attributable to the sofa. The difference between the cash price and the total payment stream is interest revenue, and Somnolent should record it under the effective interest method over the two-year payment period.

Barter Transactions

A transaction does not generate revenue if it involves the exchange of goods or services of a similar nature or value. If the exchange is for dissimilar goods or services, the transaction does create revenue; this is measured at the fair value of the goods or services received, as modified by the amount of any cash transferred. If the fair value of received goods or services cannot be reliably measured, then use instead the fair value of the goods or services given up, as modified by the amount of any cash transferred.

Revenue Components

If a revenue transaction can be split into separately identifiable components, then each component should be dealt with separately in order to reflect the substance of the transaction. Thus, the later-period servicing portion of a sales transaction should be segregated from the rest of the transaction and recognized over the performance period.

Goods Repurchases

If an entity enters into multiple transactions whose effect on revenue is best understood when viewed together, then it should judge the transactions as a whole. For example, one transaction to sell goods and another transaction to repurchase the same goods at a later date should be dealt with as a non–revenue-generating activity.

REVENUE TIMING FOR GOODS

Basic Principle of Revenue Timing

Revenue should be recognized when it is probable that future economic benefits will flow to the entity, and the benefits can be measured reliably.

Sale of Goods

Revenue from the sale of goods can be recognized when *all* of the following conditions have been recognized.

- **Benefits assured.** The economic benefits associated with the transaction will flow to the entity.

- **Costs measurable.** The costs related to the transaction can be reliably measured.
- **Ownership relinquished.** The entity no longer retains management control over the goods sold.
- **Revenue measurable.** The amount of revenue to be recognized can be reliably measured.
- **Risks and rewards transferred.** All significant risks and rewards associated with the goods have been transferred to the buyer. This usually coincides with the transfer of legal title or possession to the buyer.

The economic benefits of a transaction may not be assured until the entity receives the consideration it is due, or an uncertainty is removed. If so, it cannot recognize revenue until these conditions have been met.

Example

Bright Star Corporation has manufactured an advanced telescope that is built to withstand extremely cold temperatures, for use at a South Pole observatory. Bright Star has manufactured the device specifically for the nonprofit organization operating the observatory, and it is unlikely that the device could be used elsewhere in the world. Bright Star has not manufactured a telescope before for this environment and so expects a number of problems to arise during its first year of operation. Bright Star is contractually obligated to correct any such problems that arise during the first year of use.

Given the high risk of significant extra costs being incurred, and Bright Star's inability to quantify these costs, it should not recognize any revenue until the contract period has expired.

Retention of Ownership Risk

If an entity retains significant risks of ownership in ostensibly transferred goods, then it cannot recognize related revenue. Examples of significant retained ownership risks are

- **Contingent conditions.** The buyer of the goods must in turn sell the goods before it pays the entity for the sale.
- **Installation conditions.** Installation is a significant part of the contract, and it has not yet been completed. The seller can recognize revenue immediately after the buyer accepts delivery if the installation process is simple, or when the inspection is performed only for purposes of final determination of contract prices.
- **Performance obligations.** The entity retains an obligation for unsatisfactory performance that exceeds normal warranty provisions.
- **Return rights.** The buyer is entitled to rescind the purchase, and the probability of such return is uncertain. The seller can recognize rev-

enue when the buyer has formally accepted delivery or when the time period allowed for rejection has expired.

Example

Florentine Flatware sells its tableware through the Upper Crust retail chain. Upper Crust purchases tableware from Florentine under a consignment agreement. Florentine should recognize revenue from the sale of its tableware only when the goods are sold by Upper Crust.

If an entity retains an insignificant risk of ownership, it can recognize revenue. For example, if an entity has transferred the significant risks and rewards of ownership, except for legal title in order to protect collectibility, then revenue may be recognized. Similarly, a retail establishment can recognize revenue even when customers have a refund right, as long as the retailer can reliably estimate future returns and recognizes a related liability.

Cash-on-Delivery Transactions

If a seller is selling goods based on cash-on-delivery terms, then it should recognize revenue when it delivers the goods and collects the cash from the transaction.

Subscriptions

When the seller makes deliveries of publications and similar items to the buyer under a subscription agreement, it normally recognizes revenue on a straight-line basis over the period when the items are issued. However, if the items vary in value by period, then the seller should recognize revenue based on the sale value of each item in proportion to the total estimated sales value of all items included in the subscription.

Advance Payments

The buyer may send either full or partial payment to the seller in advance of the delivery of goods. The seller may not yet have the items in inventory, they may still be in the production process, or they will be drop shipped by a third party. Under these circumstances, the seller should not recognize revenue until the goods are delivered to the buyer.

Installment Sales

The buyer may send a series of payments to the seller in exchange for the immediate delivery of goods from the seller to the buyer. In this case, the seller can recognize revenue once the goods are delivered; however, the amount recognized is the present value of all payments, which the seller calculates by discounting the payments at the imputed rate of interest.

The seller recognizes the interest portion of the payments as it earns them, which it calculates using the effective interest method.

Layaway Sales

Layaway sales occur when goods are delivered to the buyer only when the buyer has completed the final payment in a series of installment payments. In a layaway sale, the seller recognizes revenue only when it delivers the goods. However, if the seller's historical experience shows that most layaway transactions are converted into sales, then it can recognize revenue when it receives a significant deposit, provided that the goods are on hand, identified, and ready for delivery. Some features of this transaction are similar to bill-and-hold transactions, which are discussed next.

Bill-and-Hold Transactions

In a bill-and-hold sale, the buyer requests that delivery be delayed, but accepts billing and takes title to the goods. The seller recognizes revenue when the buyer takes title and these conditions are satisfied:

- Normal payment terms apply to the transaction;
- The buyer acknowledges the delayed delivery instructions;
- It is probable that delivery will be made; and
- The goods are identified, on hand and ready for delivery.

The seller cannot recognize revenue related to a bill-and-hold transaction if there is only an intention to acquire or produce the goods in time for delivery, as opposed to actually being on hand.

Sale-and-Repurchase Transactions

A sale-and-repurchase agreement arises when the seller concurrently agrees to repurchase the same goods at a later date, or when either party has an option to force the seller to repurchase the goods. If the seller has transferred the risks and rewards of ownership to the buyer, then the seller can recognize revenue. Alternatively, if the seller has retained the risks and rewards of ownership, even if legal title has been transferred, then the transaction is instead treated as a financing arrangement and does not generate revenue.

Sales to Intermediate Parties

When a seller transfers goods to distributors or dealers for resale, the seller can recognize revenue when the risks and rewards of ownership have passed to the buyer. If not, the buyer is really an agent, and the seller therefore cannot recognize revenue until such time as a third party acquires the goods from the agent.

Revenue and Expense Matching

An entity should recognize the revenue and expenses associated with the same transaction at the same time. However, it cannot recognize revenue when the associated expenses cannot be reliably measured. Instead, the entity should record any consideration already received as a liability, until such time as the matching expense amounts can be reliably measured and recorded.

REVENUE MEASUREMENT FOR SERVICES

Percentage of Completion

An entity may recognize service revenue based on the stage of completion, which is called the *percentage-of-completion method.* This allows for the recognition of revenue in those accounting periods when the entity performs services. The percentage of completion can be derived using any of the following methods:

- Surveys of work completed
- Services performed for the contract to date, as a percentage of total services to be performed under the contract
- The proportion of costs incurred to date to the estimated total cost to be incurred under the contract

REVENUE TIMING FOR SERVICES

Sale of Services

An entity is usually able to make reliable revenue estimates after the parties to the transaction have agreed to the terms of settlement, consideration to be exchanged, and each party's rights regarding services to be provided and received. An entity can recognize the revenue associated with services provided when it satisfies all of the following conditions:

- **Revenue measurable.** The amount of revenue to be recognized can be reliably measured.
- **Benefits assured.** The economic benefits associated with the transaction will flow to the entity.
- **Completion measurable.** The stage of completion at the end of the reporting period can be reliably measured.
- **Costs measurable.** The costs related to the transaction can be reliably measured, as can the costs to complete it.

Progress payments or advances paid to date by customers do not necessarily relate to the proportion of work completed and so cannot be used as a basis for revenue recognition.

The following issues also apply to the recognition of revenue related to the provision of services.

- **Straight-line recognition.** If the services provided are comprised of an indeterminate number of acts over a specified period of time, revenue should be recognized on a straight-line basis over the designated time period, unless some other method better represents the provision of services.
- **Significant activities.** If a specific activity is substantially more significant than other activities, then an entity should defer revenue recognition until that activity has been completed.
- **Unreliable estimates.** When an entity cannot reliably estimate the outcome of services, it should recognize revenue only to the extent of the expenses recognized that are recoverable. Under this scenario, no profit is recognized. If it is not probable that the costs incurred are recoverable, then the entity does not recognize revenue and it recognizes all costs incurred as expenses.

Admission Fees

The fees generated from artistic performances and other special events are recognized when the event takes place. If the seller is selling subscriptions to a number of events, then it allocates the subscription to each event covered by the subscription, based on the extent to which services are performed at each event.

Commissions

Commissions can be earned for a variety of transactions. Here are the recognition criteria for several types of commissions.

- **Advertising.** An advertising agency can recognize commissions when the related advertisements are released. If it earns commissions for production work, it recognizes revenue based on the stage of completion of the project.
- **Financial services.** Revenue recognition of fees earned for financial services requires the seller to distinguish among
  - Fees that are really part of the interest rate of a financial instrument, which should be treated as an adjustment to the effective interest rate.

- Fees earned for services to be rendered, such as a loan servicing fee or an investment management fee.
- Fees earned upon the completion of a significant act, such as a loan placement fee or a loan syndication fee.

- **Insurance.** An insurance agent is not normally obligated to render further services once the policy commences. If so, the agent can recognize the commission as revenue on the policy commencement date. If the agent is required to render further services during the policy period, then the agent must recognize the commission over the policy period.

Franchise Fees

Franchise fees are recognized based on the purpose for which they were charged. The following types of fee recognition can be used.

- **Assets.** The franchisor recognizes fees as revenue either when it delivers assets to franchisees or when it transfers title.
- **Services.** The franchisor recognizes revenue associated with continuing services over the period during which the services are rendered. If the related fee is not sufficient to cover the franchisor's provisioning costs and a reasonable profit, then it must defer the necessary additional amount from its initial franchise fee and recognize it as revenue over the servicing period. The franchisor can recognize the remainder of any initial fee when it has performed all of its obligations to the franchisee.
- **Continuing franchise fees.** When the franchisor charges a fee for various continuing rights or services, it recognizes revenue over the applicable period.
- **Agency transactions.** If the franchisor acts as an agent for a franchisee, such as when it orders supplies on behalf of the franchisee at no profit, this transaction cannot be recognized as revenue.

If franchise fees are collectible over an extended period and there is significant collection uncertainty, then the franchisor recognizes revenue as it collects cash installments.

If the franchisor's obligations under an area franchise agreement depend on the number of outlets established, revenue recognition should be based on the proportion of outlets for which services have been substantially completed.

Initiation and Membership Fees

If an initiation or membership fee only creates a membership condition, then the seller can recognize revenue when there is no significant uncertainty regarding fee collectibility. However, if the fee entitles the buyer to services or publications or discounted purchases from the seller during the membership period, then the seller recognizes revenue on a basis that reflects the timing, nature, and value of the benefits provided.

Installation Fees

When a seller charges an installation fee associated with a delivery of goods, the seller recognizes revenue in accordance with the stage of completion of the installation. However, if the installation fee is incidental to the sale of goods, then the fee is recognized when the goods are sold.

Servicing Fees

A seller of goods may include in the selling price a fee for subsequent servicing or product upgrades. If so, the seller should defer the amount of revenue related to the servicing fee, which should cover the servicing cost and a reasonable profit. It should then recognize the associated revenue over the servicing period.

Software Development Fees

If an entity accepts fees for developing customized software for a client, then it recognizes revenue based on the stage of completion of the software development process; this includes any further services provided to the client for subsequent product support.

Tuition Fees

The provider of educational services should recognize revenue from tuition fees over the period of instruction.

CONSTRUCTION CONTRACTS

A construction contract is typically negotiated for the construction of a single asset, such as a bridge, building, or dam, but can also involve the destruction or restoration of assets. It also includes the rendering of related services, such as project management and architectural design. Construction contracts are typically of considerable duration, so revenue can be recognized over multiple accounting periods. Thus, revenue recognition involves the proper allocation of revenue to each accounting period in which construction work is performed.

Separation and Aggregation of Contracts

When a contract covers a number of assets, treat the construction of each asset as a separate contract when

- Separate proposals were submitted for each asset;
- Each asset was subject to separate negotiation; and
- The revenues and costs associated with each asset can be identified.

When there is a group of construction contracts, treat them as a single contract when

- The contracts were negotiated as a single package;
- The contracts are, in effect, part of a single project; and
- The contracts are performed concurrently or in a continuous sequence.

If a contract provides for construction of additional assets at the customer's option, treat the extra work as a separate contract when the asset differs in design or function from the assets in the original contract and the price of the additional work is negotiated separately from the original contract price.

Contract Revenue Inclusions

The contractor can recognize revenue that is included in the contract as well as additional claims and incentive payments to the extent that they will probably result in revenue and can be reliably measured.

The contractor measures revenue at the fair value of the consideration paid. This measurement is subject to some uncertainty, given the extent of ongoing changes in claims, project scope, cost escalation clauses, and penalties. Claims arise from such issues as customer delays and specification errors, and so are particularly subject to outcome variation, depending on the outcome of negotiations. Given these issues, revenue estimates may vary considerably from period to period.

Contract Revenue Recognition

The contractor can recognize the revenues and expenses associated with a contract, through the stage of completion of the contract at the end of the current reporting period (the *percentage-of-completion method*), when it can reliably estimate the outcome of the contract.

If the contract is fixed price, the contractor can consider the contract's outcome to be reliably estimated when the following four conditions are satisfied:

1. All contract revenue can be reliably measured.
2. The benefits of the contract will probably flow to the contractor.
3. The remaining contract costs and the stage of completion at the end of the reporting period can be reliably measured.

4. Costs attributable to the contract can be identified and reliably measured, so that costs actually incurred can be compared to prior cost estimates.

If the contract is cost plus, the contractor can consider the contract's outcome to be reliably estimated when the following two conditions are satisfied:

1. The benefits of the contract will probably flow to the contractor.
2. Contract costs, whether reimbursable or not, can be reliably measured.

If the contractor cannot reliably estimate the outcome of a contract, then it can recognize revenue only to the extent of contract costs incurred that it will probably recover, with no profit recognition.

Under the percentage-of-completion method, the contractor matches revenues with contract costs incurred in reaching a designated stage of completion; this results in the reporting of both revenue and expenses that can be attributed to the proportion of work completed. If the contractor has incurred costs that relate to future contract activity, then it categorizes these costs as an asset designated as Contract Work-in-Progress.

A contractor can use a variety of methods to determine the stage of completion of a contract, including the following:

• Surveys of work performed.
• Completion of a physical proportion of the work.
• The contract costs incurred to date as a percentage of the estimated total contract costs. This calculation should exclude contract costs related to future activity on a contract and payments made to subcontractors in advance of work performed.

Example

Hephaestus Construction, builder of Greek-style homes, is working on a contract for Ms. Hestia, involving a main house and guest house. The first segment of the contract is for the main house. Hephaestus spends €180,000 for building materials that have been delivered to the construction site, but which are designated for the guest house, for which no work has yet begun. Hephaestus has also made an advance payment of €25,000 to Poseidon Concrete for the construction of an Olympic-size swimming pool. In both cases, Hephaestus cannot include the expense in its percentage-of-completion calculations, since they do not reflect work performed to date.

The percentage-of-completion method involves making ongoing changes in accounting estimates. As such, changes in estimate are recognized in the period in which the change is made and in subsequent periods; the method does not alter the accounting in prior periods.

Example

Eagle Construction enters into a fixed price contract with Avignon Prefecture to build a suspension bridge. The amount of revenue listed in the contract is €5,800,000. Eagle's initial estimate of project costs is €5,000,000 over the expected three-year term of the project.

At the end of Year 1, Eagle revises its estimate of project costs upward to €5,100,000.

In Year 2, Avignon approves a change in the contract scope to include temperature sensors on the bridge surface that will transmit a warning when the road temperature drops below freezing. The scope change calls for a revenue increase of €300,000, and Eagle estimates additional contract costs of €250,000. At the end of that year, Eagle has spent €150,000 for materials that are stored at the construction site, but which are intended for use in the following year.

Eagle calculates its revenue recognition based on the percentage-of-completion method. A summary of its calculations follows.

	Year 1	Year 2	Year 3
Initial revenue in contract	€5,800,000	€5,800,000	€5,800,000
Contract scope changes	—	300,000	300,000
Total contract revenue	€5,800,000	€6,100,000	€6,100,000
Costs incurred to date	1,785,000	4,013,000	5,350,000
Estimated costs to complete	3,315,000	1,337,000	—
Total estimated contract costs	5,100,000	5,350,000	5,350,000
Estimated profit	€700,000	€750,000	€750,000
Stage of completion	40%	80%	100%

Eagle calculates the 80% stage of completion at the end of Year 2 without the €150,000 of contract costs related to materials stored for use in Year 3.

Based on the preceding information, Eagle recognizes revenue and expenses by year in the following amounts:

	Project to Date	Prior Years Recognition	Current Year Recognition
Year 1			
Revenue (€5,800,000 × 40%)	€2,320,000	—	€2,320,000
Expenses (€5,100,000 × 40%)	2,040,000	—	2,040,000
Profit	280,000	—	280,000
Year 2			
Revenue (€6,100,000 × 80%)	4,880,000	€2,320,000	2,560,000
Expenses (€5,350,000 × 80%)	4,280,000	2,040,000	2,240,000
Profit	600,000	280,000	320,000
Year 3			
Revenue (€6,100,000 × 100%)	6,100,000	4,880,000	1,220,000
Expenses (€5,350,000 × 100%)	5,350,000	4,280,000	1,070,000
Profit	750,000	600,000	150,000

Recognition of Expected Losses

The contractor should recognize an expected loss immediately when it is probable that total contract costs will exceed total contract revenue. The amount of the loss recognized is not impacted by the stage of project completion or the amount of profits that the contractor may earn from contracts that are not treated as part of the same contract. Examples of situations where contract recoverability is in doubt are

- Contracts that are not enforceable.
- Contracts that are subject to litigation or legislation.
- Contracts for property that are likely to be condemned or expropriated.
- Contracts where the customer is unlikely to meet its obligations.
- Contracts where the contractor cannot meet its obligations.

When an uncertainty arises about the collectibility of an amount already recognized in revenue, the contractor records the uncollectible amount as an expense rather than as a downward adjustment of contract revenue.

Agreements for the Construction of Real Estate

An entity may undertake the construction of real estate and then enter into agreements with one or more buyers before construction is complete. This may involve payment of an initial deposit, possibly with additional progress payments, with a final payment due on contractual completion of the project. The buyer then takes possession of the real estate.

In the sales contract, the entity may agree to also provide goods or services as well as to construct the real estate. If so, the entity must allocate the consideration into separate components for revenue recognition purposes, using the fair value of the total consideration in the contract. If revenue itemized in the contract must be split in this manner, there are three possible scenarios to consider.

1. **Treatment as a construction contract.** Revenue recognition is in accordance with the stage of completion, using the percentage-of-completion method.

2. **Treatment as the sale of goods.** This option applies if the buyer has only limited ability to influence the design of the real estate or to specify only minor variations to the basic design. If the entity transfers control over the real estate at a single time, such as on completion, then the entity only recognizes revenue at that time. If the entity transfers control as construction progresses, then it can recognize revenue under the percentage-of-completion method.

3. **Treatment for the rendering of services.** If the entity is not required to acquire and supply construction materials, then revenue recognition as if that portion of the contract were for services is appropriate. The appropriate accounting for services was addressed earlier in the "Revenue Measurement for Services" section and the "Revenue Timing for Services" section.

If the entity must provide additional work on real estate already delivered to the buyer, it must recognize a liability for the amount of revenue allocated to that portion of the work and may recognize it as revenue on completion of the various stages of additional work.

Example

Modigliani & Sons buys a plot of land, designs an office building to be situated on the land, and obtains all necessary building permits. It then enters into a contract with Berlitz Partners to sell it the plot of land and to construct the building. Modigliani can recognize the revenue associated with the land immediately.

Since Modigliani already obtained approval for the office building, it can assume there will be few changes to the building design once construction has begun. Thus, that portion of the contract associated with the construction of the building is considered a sale of goods. Since the building is being constructed on land now owned by Berlitz, it is reasonable to assume that Berlitz is taking control of the building as construction progresses, so Modigliani should recognize revenue related to the building construction under the percentage-of-completion method.

Alternatively, if Berlitz had the right to put the building back to Modigliani prior to its completion, then Modigliani would really transfer control only on project completion, so it would recognize all revenue related to building construction only on completion of the project.

If an entity not only constructs real estate but also engages in a considerable amount of ongoing managerial involvement in the property, then a case can be made that the risks and rewards of ownership are not transferred to the buyer even on the completion of construction. This situation can arise when the entity guarantees occupancy of the property or a return on the buyer's investment for a certain period of time. Such situations may call for the further delay of revenue recognition until the entity's further obligations have been resolved.

INTEREST, ROYALTIES, AND DIVIDENDS

When an entity generates revenue from the use of a third party of the entity's assets, it shall recognize revenue under the following rules:

- **Interest income,** using the effective interest method. If interest has accrued prior to the acquisition of an interest-bearing investment, the entity should allocate the subsequent receipt of interest between the preacquisition and postacquisition periods, with only the postacquisition portion recognized as revenue.
- **Royalties,** in accordance with the terms of the relevant agreement, unless the substance of the agreement calls for a different method. From a practical perspective, recognition may be on a straight-line basis over the term of the agreement. If the agreement is an assignment of rights in exchange for a fixed fee or nonrefundable guarantee where the licensor has no remaining performance obligations, the licensor can recognize revenue at the time of sale. If payment under the agreement is contingent on the occurrence of a future event, revenue should be recognized when it is probable that the fee or royalty will be received.
- **Dividends,** when the shareholder's right to receive payment is authorized.

These rules shall be used only if the amount of revenue can be reliably measured and it is probable that the benefits associated with the transaction will flow to the entity.

INCOME RECOGNITION FOR AGRICULTURAL PRODUCTS

The recognition of income related to agricultural products differs substantially from revenue recognition for most other types of business transaction, because it is based on the fair value of an entity's agricultural products.

The definition of agricultural products is quite diverse, including the raising of livestock, forestry, crop production, cultivating orchards, floriculture, and fish farming. An activity is considered to be agricultural in nature if living animals and plants are capable of biological transformation, if management facilitates that transformation, and if the change in quality or quantity caused by biological transformation can be measured and monitored as a routine management function.

Assignment of Value to Agricultural Assets

An entity shall recognize a biological asset or agricultural produce when it controls the asset, future benefits associated with the asset will probably flow to the entity, and the asset's fair value or cost can be reliably measured.

An entity shall measure its biological assets at the end of each reporting period at its fair value minus costs to sell. If fair value cannot be reliably measured, then the entity shall measure its biological assets at their cost, less accumulated depreciation and impairment losses. If a biological asset becomes reliably measurable, the entity shall value it at its fair value minus costs to sell. Agricultural produce that has been harvested shall be measured at its fair value less costs to sell as of the harvesting date.

If an entity enters into a contract to sell its biological assets or agricultural produce at a future date, it shall not use the prices in the contracts to value its assets, since these terms may be onerous. Instead, it should use the quoted prices in an active market for its assets. If there are prices available from multiple active markets, the entity should use prices existing in the market that it expects to use.

If there is no active market, then an entity shall use one of the following methods to determine fair value:

- The most recent market transaction price, provided that there have not been significant changes in economic circumstance since the date of the last price.
- Market prices for similar assets, adjusted to reflect any differences between them and the entity's assets.
- Sector benchmarks expressed as a standard unit of measure.

If no fair value information is available, then the entity may use the present value of expected net cash flows to determine the value of its assets, using the current market interest rate as the discount rate. These expected net cash flows should incorporate the entity's expectations for variations in cash flows.

Recognition of Gains and Losses

An entity shall recognize a gain or loss arising from the difference between the fair values of its biological assets less costs to sell in the current reporting period versus the preceding reporting period. A gain or loss may also arise upon the initial recognition of a biological asset. The entity shall recognize these gains or losses in the period in which they arise.

An entity shall measure the fair value of agricultural produce, less costs to sell, at the point of harvest. Once harvested, no further fair value adjustment for agricultural produce shall be made.

GOVERNMENT GRANTS

An entity shall recognize the fair value of a government grant, less costs to sell, only when the grant becomes receivable. If the grant is conditional, the entity shall recognize the grant only when it has met all of the conditions attached to the grant. If the grant allows for some degree of funds retention due to the passage of time, then the entity can recognize that portion of the grant as the requisite time periods pass.

BARTER TRANSACTIONS INVOLVING ADVERTISING SERVICES

A company may enter into a barter transaction to provide advertising services in exchange for receiving advertising services from its customer. This can involve the exchange of no cash at all or approximately equal amounts of cash or other consideration. Two forms of revenue recognition can arise from this scenario:

1. **Similar services.** If there is an exchange of similar advertising services, then the exchange does not result in revenue recognition by either party.
2. **Dissimilar services.** If there is an exchange of dissimilar advertising services, the seller can recognize revenue. It is not allowable to do so based on the fair value of advertising services received. Instead, the seller can measure revenue based on the fair value of the advertising services it provides, by reference to nonbarter transactions that

    a. Involve advertising similar to that included in the barter transaction;
    b. Occur frequently;
    c. Involve a different counterparty than in the barter transaction;
    d. Involve cash or other consideration that has a reliably measurable fair value; and
    e. Represent a predominant number of transactions and amounts as compared to the barter transaction.

Example

Stoked TV enters into an advertising barter transaction with *Dude* magazine, where Stoked advertises *Dude* on its cable network in exchange for similar coverage in *Dude* magazine. Stoked is providing *Dude* with five advertising spots of 30 seconds' duration. Stoked normally provides such coverage at a rate of $10,000 per spot and does so frequently with other parties, who pay cash. The proportion of transactions where Stoked is paid cash for advertising is approximately 90% of all of its advertising transactions. Accordingly, Stoked TV can recognize the fair value of its advertising as revenue, which is $10,000 multiplied by five coverage spots, or $50,000.

CUSTOMER LOYALTY PROGRAMS

A customer loyalty program is used by a company to give its customers an incentive to buy its goods or services. Customers earn award credits by buying from the company, which they can then use to obtain free or discounted goods or services.

A company that issues award credits shall treat them as a separately identifiable component of the sales transaction in which they are granted. The company must allocate the sale between the award credits and the other components of the sale. The amount of the allocation to the award credits shall be based on the fair value of credits, which is the price at which the credits can be sold separately or the fair value of the awards for which they can be redeemed. In the latter case, the fair value of the awards should be reduced to account for the proportion of award credits that the company does not expect its customers to redeem. If customers can select from a number of awards, then the fair value analysis should reflect an average of the award fair values, weighted for the frequency of expected award selection. If an allocation of consideration to award credits is not possible based on fair values, a company may use alternative methods.

If the company pays out awards itself, then it recognizes revenue for the consideration allocated to the award credits when customers redeem the awards and the company delivers the awards.

Example

Ace Auto Magic has a customer loyalty program. It grants participating customers award points every time they purchase from Ace. Customers can redeem their points for free oil changes at any Ace store. The points are valid for three years from the date of each customer's last purchase, so the points essentially have no termination date as long as customers keep buying from Ace.

During February, Ace issues 80,000 award points. Management expects that 75% of these points, or 60,000 points, will eventually be redeemed. Management estimates that the fair value of each award point is ten cents, and so defers revenue recognition on €6,000.

After one year, customers have redeemed 30,000 of the award points for oil changes, so Ace recognizes revenue of €3,000 (30,000 redeemed points / 60,000 estimated total redemptions × €6,000 deferred revenue).

During the second year, management revises its redemption estimate, and now expects that 70,000 of the original 80,000 award points will be redeemed. During that year, 20,000 points are redeemed, so that a total of 50,000 points have now been redeemed. The cumulative revenue that Ace recognizes is €4,286 (50,000 redeemed points / 70,000 estimated total redemptions × €6,000 deferred revenue). Since Ace already recognized €3,000 in Year 1, it now recognizes €1,286 in Year 2.

During the third year, customers redeem an additional 20,000 award points, which brings total redemptions to 70,000. Management does not expect additional redemptions. Accordingly, Ace recognizes the remainder of the deferred revenue, which is €1,714.

If a third party pays out the awards, the company is essentially collecting the consideration allocated to the awards on behalf of the third party. In this scenario, the company measures its revenue as the difference between the consideration allocated to the award credits and the amount payable to the third party for supplying the awards. The company can recognize this net difference as revenue as soon as the third party becomes obligated to supply awards and is entitled to be paid for doing so. This recognition may arise as soon as the company grants award credits. However, if customers can claim awards from either the company or the third party, revenue recognition only occurs when customers claim awards.

Example

Organic Delights, a purveyor of organically grown farm produce, participates in the customer loyalty program operated by Dakota Airlines. Organic grants its participating customers one air travel point for every euro they spend on farm produce. These customers can then redeem the points for air travel with Dakota. Organic pays Dakota €0.008 for each point. During the first year of the program's operation, Organic awards 3 million points.

Organic estimates that the fair value of an award point is €0.01. It therefore allocates to the 3 million issued points €30,000 of the consideration it has received from the sale of its produce. Organic has no further obligation to its customers, since Dakota is now obligated to supply the awards. Accordingly, Organic can recognize the €30,000 of revenue allocated to the award points at once as well as the €24,000 expense payable to Dakota (€3,000,000 × €0.008).

If Organic had acted as an agent for Dakota and simply collected funds on behalf of Dakota, then it would recognize revenue only as the net amount it retains, which is €6,000 (€30,000 allocated to the awarded points − €24,000 paid to Dakota).

If the cost of the obligation to supply awards exceeds the consideration received, the company should recognize a liability for the excess amount. This situation can arise, for example, when the cost of supplying awards increases or when the proportion of award credits redeemed increases.

OTHER REVENUE RECOGNITION ISSUES

Bad Debts

When an uncertainty arises about the collectibility of an amount that has already been recognized as revenue, the uncollectible amount is recognized as an expense rather than a reduction of the revenue already recognized. This rule applies to revenue recognized under the sale of goods, the provision of services, and interest, royalties, and dividends.

Collections on Behalf of Third Parties

Revenue can only be recognized by an entity if the related transactions occur on its own account. For example

- **Agencies.** Amounts collected by an agent are on behalf of the principal and so do not alter the equity of the agent. These amounts are therefore not revenue; the agent should instead record commissions received as revenue.
- **Taxes.** Amounts collected on behalf of government entities, such as sales taxes and value-added taxes, do not create economic benefits for the entity and do not alter its equity; therefore, such transactions are excluded from revenue.

REVENUE RECOGNITION DISCLOSURES

General Disclosures

An entity should disclose the following items:

- **Policies.** The revenue recognition policies the entity has adopted, including the methods it uses to determine stages of completion for the provision of services.
- **Revenue categories.** The amount of revenue associated with each of the following categories:
  - Sale of goods
  - Rendering of services
  - Interest
  - Royalties
  - Dividends
- **Exchanges.** The revenue caused by exchanges of goods or services in each of the preceding categories.

Agricultural Disclosures

The following disclosures related to revenue recognition are required of an entity that engages in agricultural activity.

- **Assumptions.** The significant assumptions applied in determining the fair value of each group of agricultural produce at the point of harvest and each group of biological assets.
- **Basis of change.** Separate disclosure of the physical changes in the biological asset and price changes in the market that aggregate into the total fair value change. Both disclosures are reduced by the costs to sell.
- **Fair value.** The fair value less costs to sell of agricultural produce harvested during the period, as determined at the point of harvest.
- **Gains and losses.** The aggregate gains and losses arising during the current period on the initial recognition of biological assets and agricultural produce as well as from the change in fair value less costs to sell of biological assets.
- **Metrics.** Nonfinancial measures of the physical quantities of each group of biological assets at the end of the period and the output of agricultural produce during the period.

If an entity uses cost less accumulated depreciation and impairment losses to measure its biological assets, then it must disclose the following information:

- Asset description
- Why fair value cannot be used
- The range of estimates within which fair value is highly likely to lie
- The depreciation method and useful lives used
- The gross carrying amount and accumulated depreciation and impairment losses at the beginning and end of the period

If an entity is able to begin valuing at their fair value its biological assets, which had previously been valued at cost, it should disclose a description of the assets, explain why fair value is now reliably measurable, and the effect of the change.

If an entity has received government grants, then it must disclose the nature and extent of the grants, any unfulfilled conditions of the grants, and any expected decreases in the level of the grants.

Construction Contract Disclosures

At an aggregate level, a contractor should disclose the amount of contract revenue recognized in the period, the methods used to determine revenue, and the methods used to determine contract stages of completion.

For contracts in progress, a contractor should disclose the aggregate amount of costs incurred and recognized profits to date, the amount of advances received, and the amount of retentions (i.e., the amount of progress billings not paid until conditions in the contract have been satisfied).

The contractor shall also report as an asset the gross amount due from customers for contract work. This is the net amount of costs incurred plus recognized profits, minus the sum of recognized losses and progress billings for all contracts in progress where costs incurred plus recognized profits exceed progress billings.

The contractor shall also report as a liability the gross amount due to customers for contract work. This is the net amount of costs incurred plus recognized profits, minus the sum of recognized losses and progress billings for all contracts in progress where billings exceed costs incurred plus recognized profits.

3 REVENUE RECOGNITION WHEN COLLECTION IS UNCERTAIN

OVERVIEW

Under generally accepted accounting principles (GAAP), revenue recognition customarily does not depend on the collection of cash. Accrual accounting techniques normally record revenue at the point of a credit sale by establishing a receivable. When uncertainty arises surrounding the collectibility of this amount, the receivable is appropriately adjusted by establishing a valuation allowance. In some cases, however, the collection of the sales price may be so uncertain that an objective measure of ultimate collectibility cannot be established. When such circumstances exist, the seller uses either the installment method or the cost recovery method to recognize the transaction. Both of these methods allow for a deferral of gross profit until cash has been collected. The Accounting Principles Board specifically noted that these installment methods are "not acceptable" if revenues and a provision for uncollectible accounts can be reasonably estimated.

An installment transaction occurs when a seller delivers a product or performs a service and the buyer makes periodic payments over an extended period of time. Under the *installment method*, revenue recognition is deferred until the period(s) of cash collection. The seller recognizes both revenues and cost of sales at the time of the sale; however, the related gross profit is deferred to those periods in which cash is collected. Under the *cost recovery method,* both revenues and cost of sales are recognized at the time of the sale, but none of the related gross profit is recognized until the entire cost of sales has been recovered. Once the seller has recovered all costs of sales, any additional cash receipts are recognized as revenue. One method is not preferred over the other. However, the cost recovery method is more conservative than the installment method because gross profit is deferred until all costs have been recovered; therefore, it is more appropriate for situations of extreme uncertainty.

DEFINITIONS OF TERMS

Cost recovery method. The method of accounting for an installment basis sale whereby the gross profit is deferred until all cost of sales has been recovered.

Deferred gross profit. The gross profit from an installment basis sale that will be recognized in future periods.

Gross profit rate. The percentage computed by dividing gross profit by revenue from an installment sale.

Installment. The method of accounting for a sale whereby gross profit is recognized in each period in which cash from the sale is collected.

Installment sale. A sales transaction for which the sales price is collected through the receipt of periodic payments over an extended period of time.

Net realizable value. The portion of the recorded amount of an asset expected to be realized in cash upon its liquidation in the ordinary course of business.

Realized gross profit. The gross profit recognized in the current period.

Repossessions. Merchandise sold by a seller under an installment arrangement that the seller physically takes back after the buyer defaults on the payments.

INSTALLMENT METHOD

The installment method was developed in response to the increasing incidence of sales contracts that allowed buyers to make payments over several years. As the payment period becomes longer, the risk of loss resulting from uncollectible accounts increases; consequently, circumstances surrounding a receivable may lead to considerable uncertainty as to whether payments will actually be received. Under these circumstances, the uncertainty of cash collection dictates that revenue recognition be deferred until the actual receipt of cash.

The installment method can be used in most sales transactions for which payment is to be made through periodic installments over an extended period of time and the collectibility of the sales price cannot be reasonably estimated. This method is applicable to the sales of real estate, heavy equipment, home furnishings, and other merchandise sold on an installment basis. Installment method revenue recognition is not in accordance with accrual accounting because revenue recognition is not normally based on cash collection; however, its use is justified in certain circumstances on the grounds that accrual accounting may result in "front-end loading" (i.e., all of the revenue from a transaction being recognized at the point of sale with an improper matching of related costs). For example, the application of accrual accounting to transactions that provide for installment payments over periods of 10, 20, or 30 years may underestimate losses from contract defaults and other future contract costs.

APPLYING THE INSTALLMENT METHOD

When a seller uses the installment method, both revenue and cost of sales are recognized at the point of sale, but the related gross profit is deferred to those periods during which cash will be collected. As receivables are collected, a portion of the deferred gross profit equal to the gross profit rate times the cash collected is recognized as income. When this method is used, the seller must compute each year's gross profit rate and also must maintain records of installment accounts receivable and deferred revenue that are separately identified by the year of sale. All general and administrative expenses are normally expensed in the period incurred.

The steps to use in accounting for sales under the installment method are as follows:

1. During the current year, record sales and cost of sales in the regular manner. Record installment sales transactions separately from other sales. Set up installment accounts receivable identified by the year of sale (e.g., Installment Accounts Receivable—2010).
2. Record cash collections from installment accounts receivable. Care must be taken so that the cash receipts are properly identified as to the year in which the receivable arose.
3. At the end of the current year, transfer installment sales revenue and installment cost of sales to deferred gross profit properly identified by the year of sale. Compute the current year's gross profit rate on installment sales as follows:

$$\text{Gross profit rate} = 1 - \left(\frac{\text{Cost of installment sales}}{\text{Installment sales revenue}} \right)$$

Alternatively, the gross profit rate can be computed as follows:

$$\text{Gross profit rate} = \frac{\text{Installment sales revenue} - \text{Cost of installment sales}}{\text{Installment sales revenue}}$$

4. Apply the current year's gross profit rate to the cash collections from the current year's installment sales to compute the realized gross profit from the current year's installment sales.

$$\text{Realized gross profit} = \text{Cash collections from the current year's installment sales} \times \text{Current year's gross profit rate}$$

5. Separately apply each of the previous years' gross profit rates to cash collections from those years' installment sales to compute the realized gross profit from each of the previous years' installment sales.

$$\text{Realized gross profit} = \text{Cash collections from the previous years' installment sales} \times \text{Previous years' gross profit rate}$$

6. Defer the current year's unrealized gross profit to future years. The deferred gross profit to carry forward to future years is computed as follows:

$$\text{Deferred gross profit (2010)} = \text{Ending balance installment account receivable (2010)} \times \text{Gross profit rate (2010)}$$

Example of the installment method of accounting

	2010	2011	2012
Sales on installment	$400,000	$450,000	$600,000
Cost of installment sales	(280,000)	(337,500)	(400,000)
Gross profit on sales	$120,000	$112,500	$200,000
Cash collections:			
2010 sales	$150,000	$175,000	$ 75,000
2011 sales		$200,000	$125,000
2012 sales			$300,000

Accounting entries are made for steps 1 and 2 above using this data; the following computations are required for steps 3 through 6:

Step 3: Compute the current year's gross profit rate.

	2010	2011	2012
Gross profit on sales	$120,000	$112,500	$200,000
Installment sales revenue	$400,000	$450,000	$600,000
Gross profit rate	30%	25%	33⅓%

Step 4: Apply the current year's gross profit rate to cash collections from current year's sales.

Year	Cash collections		Gross profit rate		Realized gross profit
2010	$150,000	×	30%	=	$ 45,000
2011	200,000	×	25%	=	50,000
2012	300,000	×	33⅓%	=	100,000

Step 5: Separately apply each of the previous years' gross profit rates to cash collections from that year's installment sales.

In Year 2011

From year	Cash collections		Gross profit rate		Realized gross profit
2010	$175,000	×	30%	=	$52,500

In Year 2012

From year	Cash collections		Gross profit rate		Realized gross profit
2010	$ 75,000	×	30%	=	$22,500
2011	125,000	×	25%	=	31,250
					$53,750

Step 6: Defer the current year's unrealized gross profit to future years.

12/31/10

Deferred gross profit (2010) =
  ($400,000 − 150,000) × 30%   = $ 75,000

12/31/11

Deferred gross profit (2011) =
  ($450,000 − 200,000) × 25%   = $ 62,500
Deferred gross profit (2010) =
  ($400,000 − 150,000 − 175,000) × 30%   =   22,500
                                               $ 85,000

12/31/12

Deferred gross profit (2012) =
  ($600,000 − 300,000) × 33⅓%   = $100,000
Deferred gross profit (2011) =
  ($450,000 − 200,000 − 125,000) × 25%   =   31,250
                                               $131,250

FINANCIAL STATEMENT PRESENTATION

If installment sales transactions represent a significant portion of the company's total sales, the following three items of gross profit would, theoretically, be reported on the company's income statement:

1. Total gross profit from current year's sales
2. Realized gross profit from current year's sales
3. Realized gross profit from prior years' sales

An income statement using the previous example would be presented as follows (assume all sales are accounted for by the installment method):

Jordan Equipment Company
Partial Income Statement
For the Years Ending December 31

	2010	*2011*	*2012*
Sales	$400,000	$450,000	$600,000
Cost of sales	(280,000)	(337,500)	(400,000)
Gross profit on current year's sales	120,000	112,500	200,000
Less deferred gross profit on current year's sales	(75,000)	(62,500)	(100,000)
Realized gross profit on current year's sales	45,000	50,000	100,000
Plus gross profit realized on prior years' sales	—	52,500	53,750
Total gross profit on sales	$ 45,000	$102,500	$153,750

However, when a company recognizes only a small portion of its revenues using the installment method, the illustrated presentation of revenue and gross profit may be confusing. Therefore, in practice, some companies simply report the realized gross profit from installment sales by displaying it as a single line item on the income statement as follows:

Stevens Furniture Company
Partial Income Statement
For the Year Ended December 31, 2010

Sales	$ 2,250,000
Cost of sales	(1,350,000)
Gross profit on sales	900,000
Gross profit realized on installment sales	35,000
Total gross profit on sales	$ 935,000

The balance sheet presentation of installment accounts receivable depends on whether installment sales are a normal part of operations. If a company sells most of its products on an installment basis, installment accounts receivable are classified as a current asset because the operating cycle of the business (the length of which is to be disclosed in the notes to the financial statements) is the average period of time covered by its installment contracts. If installment sales are not a normal part of operations, installment accounts receivable that are not to be collected for more than a year (or the length of the company's operating cycle, if different than a year) are reported as noncurrent assets. In all cases, to avoid confusion, it is desirable to fully disclose the year of maturity next to each group of installment accounts receivable as illustrated by the following example:

Current assets:

Accounts receivable		
Customers	$180,035	
Less allowance for uncollectible accounts	(4,200)	
	175,835	
Installment accounts—collectible in 2011	26,678	
Installment accounts—collectible in 2012	42,234	$244,747

Deferred gross profit is not a liability. The reason is that the seller company is not obligated to pay cash or provide services to the customer. Rather, the deferral arose because of the uncertainty surrounding the collectibility of the sales price. However, in practice, deferred gross profit is generally presented either as unearned revenue classified in the current liability section of the balance sheet or as a deferred credit displayed between liabilities and equity.

The current asset section would be presented as follows (using information from the Jordan Equipment example and assuming a 12/31/12 balance sheet):

Installment accounts receivable	(2011)	$125,000		
Installment accounts receivable	(2012)	300,000	$ 425,000	
Less: Deferred gross profit	(2011)	$ 31,250		
Deferred gross profit	(2012)	100,000	(131,250)	$293,750

INTEREST ON INSTALLMENT METHOD RECEIVABLES

The previous examples ignored interest, a major component of most installment sales contracts. It is customary for the seller to charge interest to the buyer on the unpaid installment receivable balance. Generally, installment contracts call for equal payments, each with an amount attributable to interest on the unpaid balance and the remainder to the installment receivable balance. As the maturity date nears, a smaller amount of each installment payment is attributable to interest and a larger amount is attributable to principal. Therefore, to determine the amount of gross profit to recognize, the interest must first be deducted from the installment payment, and then the difference (representing the principal portion of the payment) is multiplied by the gross profit rate as follows:

Realized gross profit = (Installment payment – Interest portion) × Gross profit rate

The interest portion of the installment payment is recorded as interest revenue at the time of the cash receipt. Appropriate accounting entries are required to accrue interest revenue when the collection dates do not correspond with the period-end.

To illustrate the accounting for installment sales contracts involving interest, assume that Genrich Equipment Company sells a machine for

$5,000 on December 31, 2009, to a customer with a dubious credit history. The machine cost Genrich $3,750. The terms of the agreement require a $1,000 down payment on the date of the sale. The remaining $4,000 is payable in equal annual installments of $1,401.06, including 15% annual interest, at the end of each of the next four years.

For each payment it receives, Genrich must compute the portion to record as interest revenue with the remaining portion of the payment (the principal) to be applied to reduce the installment account receivable balance. Gross profit is recognized only on the principal portion of each payment that is applied to reduce the installment receivable balance. The following schedule illustrates that gross profit is recognized on the entire down payment (which contains no element of interest revenue), whereas the annual installment payments are separated into their interest and principal portions, with gross profit being recognized only on the latter portion.

Schedule of Cash Receipts

Date	Cash *(debit)*	Interest revenue *(credit)*	Installment accounts receivable *(credit)*	Installment accounts receivable *balance*	Realized *gross profit*
12/31/09				$5,000.00	
12/31/09	$1,000.00	$ —	$1,000.00	4,000.00	$ 250.00[a]
12/31/10	1,401.06	600.00[b]	801.06[c]	3,198.94[d]	200.27[e]
12/31/11	1,401.06	479.84	921.22	2,277.72	230.31
12/31/12	1,401.06	341.66	1,059.40	1,218.32	264.85
12/31/13	1,401.06	182.74	1,218.32	—	304.57
	$6,604.24	$1,604.24	$5,000.00		
			Total realized gross profit		$1,250.00

Gross profit rate = 1 − ($3,750/5,000) = 25%

[a] *$1,000 × 25% = $250*
[b] *$4,000 × 15% = $600*
[c] *$1,401.06 − 600 = $801.06*
[d] *$4,000 − 801.06 = $3,198.94*
[e] *$801.06 × 25% = $200.27*

BAD DEBTS AND REPOSSESSIONS

The standard accounting treatment for uncollectible accounts is to accrue a bad debt loss in the year of sale by estimating the amount expected to be uncollectible. This treatment is consistent with the accrual and matching concepts. However, just as revenue recognition under the accrual basis is sometimes abandoned for certain installment-basis sales, the accrual basis of recognizing bad debts is also sometimes abandoned.

When the installment method is used, it is usually appropriate to recognize bad debts by the direct write-off method (i.e., bad debts are not recognized until the receivable has been determined to be uncollectible). This practice is acceptable because most installment contracts contain a provision that allows the seller to repossess the merchandise when the buyer defaults on the installment payments. The loss on the account may be eliminated or reduced because the seller has the option of reselling the repossessed merchandise. To write off an uncollectible installment receivable, the following three steps are followed:

1. The installment account receivable and the deferred gross profit are eliminated.
2. The repossessed merchandise is recorded as used inventory at its net realizable value. Net realizable value is resale value less any selling or reconditioning costs. The repossessed asset is recorded at this fair value because any asset acquired is recorded at the best approximation of its fair value.
3. Bad debt expense and a gain or loss on repossession are recognized. The bad debt expense or repossession gain or loss is the difference between the unrecovered cost (Installment account receivable–Deferred gross profit) and the net realizable value of the repossessed merchandise.

To illustrate, assume that Marcie Company determined that a $3,000 installment receivable is uncollectible. The deferred gross profit ratio on the original sale was 30%; thus, $900 deferred gross profit exists ($3,000 × 30%). If the repossessed equipment has a $1,500 net realizable value, a $600 repossession loss (or bad debt expense) should be recorded.

Installment account receivable	$ 3,000
Less deferred gross profit	(900)
Unrecovered cost	2,100
Less net realizable value of repossessed equipment	(1,500)
Repossession loss	$ 600

Marcie Company would record this loss by making the following entry:

Deferred gross profit	900	
Inventory—repossessed merchandise	1,500	
Repossession loss	600	
Installment account receivable		3,000

THE COST RECOVERY METHOD

The cost recovery method does not recognize any income on a sale until the cost of the item sold has been fully recovered through cash receipts. Once the seller has recovered all costs, any subsequent cash receipts are included in income. The cost recovery method is used when the uncertainty of collection of the sales price is so great that even use of the installment method cannot be justified.

Under the cost recovery method, both revenues and cost of sales are recognized at the point of sale, but the related gross profit is deferred until all costs of sales have been recovered. Each installment must also be divided between principal and interest, but unlike the installment method where a portion of the principal recovers the cost of sales and the remainder is recognized as gross profit, all of the principal is first applied to recover the cost of the asset sold. After all costs of sales have been recovered, any subsequent cash receipts are realized as gross profit. The cost recovery method can be illustrated by using the information from the Genrich Company example used in the section "Interest on Installment Method Receivables." If Genrich used the cost recovery method, gross profit would be realized as follows:

Schedule of Cash Receipts

Date	Cash (debit)	Deferred interest income (credit)[a]	Installment accounts receivable (credit)	Installment accounts receivable balance	Unrecovered cost	Realized gross profit	Realized interest revenue
12/31/09				$5,000.00	$3,750.00		
12/31/09	$1,000.00	$ —	$1,000.00	4,000.00	2,750.00	$ —	$ —
12/31/10	1,401.06	600.00	801.06	3,198.94	1,948.94	—	—
12/31/11	1,401.06	479.84	921.22	2,277.72	1,027.72	—	—
12/31/12	1,401.06	(31.68)	1,059.40	1,218.32	—	—	373.34[b]
12/31/13	1,401.06	(1,048.16)	1,218.32	—	—	1,250.00	1,230.90[c]
	$6,604.24		$5,000.00			$1,250.00	$1,604.24

[a] *Interest received in 2010 and 2011 is credited to deferred interest income since the cost of the asset was not recovered until 2012.*

[b] *Computed as cash received of $1,401.06 less the portion representing unrecovered cost of $1,027.72 = $373.34. Since this amount exceeds the interest paid by the customer for the year of $341.66, the remaining $31.68 reduces deferred interest income.*

[c] *Computed as cash received of $1,401.06 less the portion applied to principal of $1,218.32 = $182.74 plus the remaining deferred interest income of $1,048.16.*

The accounting entries to record the foregoing are as follows (in whole dollars):

	Debit (Credit)					
	2009	2010	2011	2012	2013	Totals
Initial sale and down payment:						
Cash	1,000					
Installment accounts receivable	4,000					
Inventory	(3,750)					
Deferred gross profit	(1,250)					

	Debit (Credit)					
	2009	2010	2011	2012	2013	Totals
Annual payments:						
Cash		1,401	1,401	1,401	1,401	5,604
Installment accounts receivable		(801)	(921)	(1,059)	(1,219)	(4,000)
Deferred interest income		(600)	(480)	32	1,048	—
Interest income				(374)	(1,230)	(1,604)
Deferred gross profit					1,250	1,250
Recognized gross profit (revenue)					(1,250)	(1,250)

DISCLOSURE OF INSTALLMENT SALES

If installment sales comprise a significant proportion of corporate sales, a footnote should disclose the revenue recognition policy used, as well as the amounts of gross profit recognized from the current and prior years, the total amount of deferred gross profit, and its placement on the balance sheet. An example is as follows:

> The company sells kitchen appliances on various installment payment plans. Given the extreme uncertainty associated with the collection of receivables under this plan, the company uses the cost recovery method to recognize profits, under which it recognizes no gross profit until all costs of goods sold have been paid back through cash receipts. In 2010, the company recognized $397,000 of gross profit earned in the current year, as well as $791,000 deferred from prior years. An additional $2,907,000 of deferred gross profits is classified as a current liability in the Unrecognized Gross Profit on Installment Sales account.

REVENUE RECOGNITION POLICIES AND PROCEDURES

It is possible to switch between use of the installment method and the cost recovery method, thereby intentionally accelerating or delaying the reported level of profitability for different receivables. To avoid this type of manipulation, an accounting policy should state that a single revenue recognition method shall be used for all installment sales.

Use the following procedure to process back into inventory any goods received as part of a repossession from an installment sale on which the customer has failed to make payments:

1. Upon the return of goods, the warehouse staff segregates the inventory and contacts the materials review board for an evaluation.
2. The materials review board periodically examines all returned goods to determine if they can be returned directly to finished goods inventory at full valuation, refurbished, or donated.

    a. If the goods are returned to finished goods stock, they are entered into inventory at full cost, and the accounting department is notified of the transaction so it can record the inventory valuation as an offset to the receivable being canceled as part of the repossession.

    b. If the goods are to be refurbished, they are entered into inventory at their current fair value, and the accounting department is notified of the reduced valuation so it can record the reduced inventory valuation as a smaller offset to the receivable being canceled as part of the repossession.

    c. If the inventory is donated, the warehouse manager fills out the Asset Donation form and sends the original to the accounting department, which retains it for use by the tax department in determining charitable donations. The accounting staff also records a full loss on the returned inventory.

3. Based on the treatment of the returned inventory, the accounting staff credits the Accounts Receivable account to eliminate the unpaid balance of the account receivable, debits the Finished Goods account for the fair value of the returned inventory, debits the Deferred Gross Profit account to eliminate the unpaid balance of unearned gross profit on the transaction, and debits the Loss on Repossessed Inventory account to charge off any difference between these entries.

REVENUE RECOGNITION CONTROLS

The gross margins associated with installment sales should be deferred until the related cash payments are received from customers. This margin is typically aggregated for all sales within a specific time period and used for all receipts related to that time period. If the gross margin percentage for a different period were to be incorrectly used to recognize gross margin dollars, there would be an impact on the reported level of profitability. The best control over this issue is a procedure clearly stating how to calculate, track, and apply gross margins when cash is received. A secondary control is a regular review of all calculations made to recognized gross margins.

4 REVENUE RECOGNITION WHEN RIGHT OF RETURN EXISTS

OVERVIEW

In some industries it is common practice for customers to have the right to return a product to the seller for a credit or refund. However, for companies that experience a high ratio of returned merchandise to sales, the recognition of the original sale as revenue is questionable. In fact, certain industries have found it necessary to defer revenue recognition until the return privilege has substantially expired. Sometimes the return privilege expires soon after the sale, as in the perishable food industry. In other cases, the return privilege may last over an extended period of time, as in textbook publishing and equipment manufacturing. The rate of return normally is directly related to the length of the return privilege. An accounting issue arises when the recognition of revenue occurs in one period while substantial returns occur in later periods.

DEFINITIONS OF TERMS

Deferred gross profit. The gross profit from a sale that is recognized in future periods because of the uncertainty surrounding the collection of the sales price.

Return privilege. A right granted to a buyer by express agreement with a seller or by customary industry practice that allows the buyer to return merchandise to the seller within a stated period of time.

REVENUE RECOGNITION WHEN THE RIGHT OF RETURN EXISTS

The following criteria are used for recognizing revenue on a sale in which a product may be returned (as a matter of contract or a matter of industry practice), either by the ultimate consumer or by a party who resells the product to others:

> *If an enterprise sells its product but gives the buyer the right to return the product, revenue from the sales transaction is recognized at the time of sale only if all of the following conditions are met:*

a. The seller's price to the buyer is substantially fixed or determinable at the date of sale.
b. The buyer has paid the seller, or the buyer is obligated to pay the seller and the obligation is not contingent on resale of the product.
c. The buyer's obligation to the seller would not be changed in the event of theft or physical destruction or damage of the product.
d. The buyer acquiring the product for resale has economic substance apart from that provided by the seller.
e. The seller does not have significant obligations for future performance to directly bring about the resale of the product by the buyer.
f. The amount of future returns can be reasonably estimated. For purposes of this statement "returns" do not include exchanges by ultimate customers of one item for another of the same kind, quality, and price.

If all of the above conditions are met, the seller recognizes revenue from the sales transaction at the time of the sale and any costs or losses expected in connection with returns are accrued. Estimated losses from contingencies should be accrued and charged to income when it is probable that an asset has been impaired or a liability incurred, and the amount of loss can be reasonably estimated.

Example of sale with right of return

Assume that Lipkis, Inc. began the sale of its new textbook on computer programming in 2010 with the following results: On December 1, 2010, 2,000 textbooks with a sales price of $45 each and total manufacturing costs of $30 each are delivered to school bookstores on account. The bookstores have the right to return the textbooks within four months of delivery date. Payment is made when the books are sold. Payments and returns for the initial deliveries are as follows:

	Cash receipts		Returns	
	Units	*Amount*	*Units*	*Amount*
November 2010				
December 2010	600	$27,000	—	—
January 2011	500	22,500	40	$1,800
February 2011	400	18,000	90	4,050
March 2011	300	13,500	30	1,350
	1,800	$81,000	160	$7,200

Lipkis, Inc. has had similar agreements with the bookstores in the past and has experienced a 15% return rate on similar sales.

If all six of the requirements were met, the following journal entries would be appropriate:

12/1/10	Accounts receivable	90,000	
	Sales (2,000 units × $45 per unit)		90,000
	To record sale of 2,000 textbooks		
12/31/10	Cash (600 units × $45 per unit)	27,000	
	Accounts receivable		27,000
	To record cash receipts for the month		
	Cost of sales	60,000	
	Inventory (2,000 units × $30 per unit)		60,000
	To record cost of goods sold for the month		
	Sales (15% × 2,000 units × $45 per unit)	13,500	
	Cost of sales (15% × 2,000 units × $30 per unit)		9,000
	Deferred gross profit on estimated returns (15% × 2,000 units × $15 per unit)		4,500
	To record estimate of returns		
1/1/11 to 3/31/11	Cash	54,000	
	Accounts receivable		54,000
	To record cash receipts		
	Inventory (160 units × $30 per unit)	4,800	
	Deferred gross profit on estimated returns	2,400	
	Accounts receivable (160 units × $45 per unit)		7,200
	To record actual returns		
3/31/11	Cost of sales (140 units × $30 per unit)	4,200	
	Deferred gross profit on estimated returns	2,100	
	Sales (140 units × $45 per unit)		6,300
	To record expiration of return privileges and adjust estimate to actual		

The revenue and cost of goods sold recognized in 2010 are based on the number of units expected to be returned, 300 (15% × 2,000 units). The net revenue recognized is $76,500 (85% × 2,000 units × $45 per unit) and the cost of goods sold recognized is $51,000 (85% × 2,000 units × $30 per unit). The deferred gross profit balance is carried forward until either the textbooks are returned or the return privilege expires.

If all of the six conditions are not met, revenue and cost of sales from the sales transactions must be deferred until either the return privilege has substantially expired or the point when all the conditions are subsequently met is reached, whichever comes first.

If the facts in the Lipkis case were altered so that the bookstores were not required to pay Lipkis until the later of the date the books were actually sold or the expiration date of the return privilege, condition b. would not be met until the store remitted payment. The following entries would be required. The return privilege is, of course, assumed to be lost by the store when the books are sold to final customers.

| 12/1/10 | Inventory on consignment | 60,000 | |
| | Inventory | | 60,000 |

To record shipment of 2,000 units to retail bookstores on consignment (2,000 units × $30 = $60,000)

| 12/31/10 | Cash (600 units × $45 per unit) | 27,000 | |
| | Sales | | 27,000 |

To record cash receipts for December

| | Cost of sales (600 units × $30 per unit) | 18,000 | |
| | Inventory on consignment | | 18,000 |

To record cost of goods sold for December

| 1/1/11 | Cash | 54,000 | |
| | Sales (1,200[a] units × $45 per unit) | | 54,000 |

To record cash receipts

| 3/31/11 | Cost of sales (1,200 units × $30 per unit) | 36,000 | |
| | Inventory on consignment | | 36,000 |

To record cost of goods sold on cash receipts

| | Inventory (160 units × $30 per unit) | 4,800 | |
| | Inventory on consignment | | 4,800 |

To record product returns

| 3/31/11 | Accounts receivable (40 units × $45 per unit) | 1,800 | |
| | Sales | | 1,800 |

To record expiration of return privilege on remaining units

| | Cost of sales (40[b] units × $30 per unit) | 1,200 | |
| | Inventory on consignment | | 1,200 |

To record cost of goods sold on products for which return privilege expired

[a] *1,800 units paid for – 600 units paid for in December*
[b] *2,000 units sold – 160 units returned – 1,800 units paid for*

DISCLOSURE OF THE RIGHT OF RETURN

If there is considerable uncertainty regarding the amount of potential sales returns, such as may be caused by a new product, potential product obsolescence, or heightened competition, then a company may be forced to not recognize any revenue at all until the right of product return has passed. Since this can cause a substantial reduction in recognized revenue, a footnote describing the reason for the recognition delay would be in order. The information in the following footnotes illustrates a sufficient level of disclosure:

1. The company is in the beta testing phase of its new crop planting system, and so has granted an unconditional right of return to the first 10 customers who have agreed to purchase the product. The right of return privilege extends for six months from the shipment date. Since there is no return history for this new product, the company has recorded the total

amount of all 10 sales in an Unearned Sales liability account, and will not recognize the revenue until the right of return period has expired. The total amount in this account is $328,000. Of this amount, $275,000 will be recognizable in March 2011, and the remaining $53,000 in May 2011, assuming that no products are returned in the interim.

2. The company's light-saber product is entirely new and is being introduced into a new market, so management feels that it cannot estimate potential levels of product returns. Consequently, the company has not recognized any revenues related to recent shipments of the product until the three-month right-of-return period has passed. The company plans to reevaluate this policy after a sufficient amount of time has passed for it to make a better estimate of potential sales returns. The initial amount of light-saber revenues that would otherwise have been recognized in the first month of shipments was $1,750,000.

RIGHT-OF-RETURN POLICIES AND PROCEDURES

Profits should not be initially overstated by the amount of any potential returns, so an accounting policy should state that a sales return allowance shall be maintained for all goods sold with the right of return.

Also, if there is a possibility that the sales department will engage in "channel stuffing" by selling more than a distribution channel can reasonably resell, another policy should state that the company shall not allow extended rights of return. This effectively eliminates one of the sales terms used to engage in channel stuffing, which is allowing customers to return unsold goods to the company for an extended period of time.

RIGHT-OF-RETURN CONTROLS

Sales returns tend not to be in pristine condition, so a company must record a write-down to their fair value at the time of the return. However, the warehouse staff tends to place them back in stock without any consideration of condition, resulting in the overstatement of finished goods inventory. A good control is to have all sales returns set to one side for review, after which they are either shifted back to stock at full value, thrown away, donated, or reclassified as used stock and assigned a reduced inventory value.

A sales return allowance is usually created that is based on a sales return history in the recent past. However, if this sales return percentage is not updated on a regular basis, the amount allocated to the allowance may diverge significantly from actual experience. Consequently, a useful control is to require ongoing verification of the amount of the return allowance against actual returns experience, preferably as part of the month-end closing procedure.

5 REVENUE RECOGNITION FOR MULTIPLE DELIVERABLES

OVERVIEW

Vendors may offer customers many related and unrelated products and services sold together ("bundled") or separately. The prices assigned to the various elements of a particular transaction or series of transactions on the seller's invoices and the timing of issuing those invoices are not always indicative of the actual earning of revenue on the various elements of these transactions. This chapter provides guidance on how to measure consideration received from complex, multielement arrangements and how to allocate that consideration between the different deliverables contained in the arrangement.

DEFINITIONS OF TERMS

Contingent amount. The portion of the total consideration to be received by a vendor under a multiple deliverable arrangement that would be realized by the vendor only if specified performance conditions were met or additional deliverables were provided to the customer.

Noncontingent amount. The portion of the total consideration to be received by a vendor under a multiple deliverable arrangement that is not subject to any additional performance requirements that the vendor must meet.

Refund rights. The legal right of a customer to obtain a concession or recover all or a portion of the consideration paid to a vendor under a multiple deliverable arrangement.

Relative fair value method. A technique for allocating the total consideration to be received by a vendor under a multiple deliverable arrangement to each separate unit of accounting based on the ratio of the fair value of each separate unit of accounting to the total fair values of all of the separate units of accounting.

Residual method. A technique for determining the portion of the total consideration to be received by a vendor under a multiple deliverable arrangement to be allocated to the units of accounting that have been delivered by subtracting the fair values of the undelivered items from the total consideration to be received.

Stand-alone value. The value that a specific product or service (deliverable) has to a customer without considering other products or services that might accompany it as part of a multiple deliverable arrangement. In order to have value to a customer on a stand-alone basis, a deliverable must be either sold separately by any vendor or be separately resalable by the customer whether or not there is an observable market for the deliverable.

Vendor-specific objective evidence (VSOE). The price that a vendor charges for a specific product or service (deliverable) when it is sold separately. If the deliverable is not currently being sold separately, a price that is established by management possessing the authority may be used under the condition that it is considered probable that the established price will not change prior to the separate market introduction of the deliverable.

OVERVIEW OF MULTIPLE DELIVERABLES REVENUE RECOGNITION

Arrangements between vendors and their customers often include the sale of multiple products and services (deliverables). A multiple deliverable arrangement (MDA) can be structured using fixed, variable, or contingent pricing or combinations thereof. Product delivery and service performance can occur at different times and in different locations, and customer acceptance can be subject to various return privileges or performance guarantees.

The key MDA revenue recognition issues are

- How a vendor determines whether an MDA consists of a single unit of accounting or multiple units of accounting.
- Allocating MDA consideration to multiple units of accounting.
- Measuring MDA consideration.

It is to be presumed that separate contracts executed at or near the same time with the same entity or related parties were negotiated as a package and are to be considered together in determining how many units of accounting are contained in an MDA. That presumption can be overcome by sufficient contradictory evidence.

Excluded from the scope of this topic are

1. Criteria for the timing of revenue recognition for a unit of accounting.
2. Arrangements in which, conditioned upon the vendor's revenue from the customer exceeding certain cumulative levels or the cus-

tomer continuing its relationship with the vendor for a specified time period,

    a. The vendor offers free or discounted products or services in the future, or

    b. The vendor provides specified future cash rebates or refunds.

3. Arrangements involving the sale of award credits, such as airline frequent-flyer or similar customer loyalty programs.

4. Accounting for the direct costs incurred by a vendor relative to an MDA.

Basic Principles

There are three basic principles, the application of which are the subject of the discussion that follows:

1. MDAs are divided into separate *units of accounting* if the deliverables included in the arrangement meet all three of the criteria presented in the table below.

2. Subject to certain limits regarding contingent amounts to be received under the MDA, *relative fair values* are used to allocate MDA proceeds to the separate units of accounting.

3. The revenue recognition criteria to be applied are determined *separately* for each unit of accounting.

Units of Accounting

The following table summarizes the criteria used in determining units of accounting for MDA:

	Criteria	*Outcome*	*Result*
1.	Does the delivered item have stand-alone value to the customer?	Yes	Go to criterion 2
		No	Do not separate item
2.	Does objective and reliable evidence exist regarding the fair value of the undelivered items?	Yes	Go to criterion 3
		No	Do not separate item
3.	If the MDA includes a general right of return with respect to the delivered item, is delivery of the undelivered items probable and substantially controlled by the vendor?	Yes or Not Applicable	Delivered item is a separate unit of accounting
		No	Do not separate item

This separability evaluation is to be applied consistently to MDAs that arise under similar circumstances or that possess similar characteristics. The evaluation is to be performed at the inception of the MDA and upon delivery of each item.

If consideration is allocated to a deliverable that does not qualify as a separate unit of accounting, then the reporting entity is required to

1. Combine the amount allocated to the deliverable with the amounts allocated to all other undelivered items included in the MDA, and
2. Determine revenue recognition for the combined items as a single unit of accounting.

Measurement and Allocation of MDA Consideration

The following decision diagram summarizes the factors to consider in measuring and allocating MDA consideration:

Measuring and Allocating MDA Consideration

The determination of whether total MDA consideration is fixed or determinable disregards the effects of refund rights or performance bonuses, if any.

After applying the criteria set forth in the decision diagram, the vendor may recognize an asset representing the cumulative difference, from inception of the MDA, between amounts recognized as revenue and amounts received or receivable from the customer (this is analogous to the asset "costs and estimated earnings in excess of billings," which is used in long-term construction accounting). The amount of such assets may not exceed the total amounts to which the vendor is legally entitled under the MDA, including fees that would be earned upon customer cancellation. The amount recognized as an asset would be further limited if the vendor did not intend to enforce its contractual rights to obtain such cancellation fees from the customer.

In measuring fair value, it is presumed that a separately stated sales price included in the sales contract for a deliverable is not representative of that deliverable's separate fair value. Rather, the best evidence of fair value is VSOE of the sales price of the deliverable on a stand-alone basis. Use of VSOE, when available, to determine fair value is always preferable. Otherwise, third-party evidence of fair value is an acceptable substitute.

Example of multiple deliverable revenue recognition

Peach Company sells an mp3 player, which it calls the Nectarine. Peach prefers to sell the Nectarine with a bundled annual support package, which sells for $320. Without the service package, the Nectarine retails for $250, and Peach sells the servicing package separately for $120 per year.

Peach splits apart the two revenue elements of the bundled annual support package by allocating revenue to the Nectarine, based on the fair values of the Nectarine and its support package, which it calculates as follows:

$$\frac{\$250 \text{ product price}}{\$250 \text{ product price} + \$120 \text{ servicing price}} \times \$320 \text{ bundled price} = \$216.22$$

Peach also allocates revenue to the support package in the same manner with the following calculation:

$$\frac{\$120 \text{ servicing price}}{\$250 \text{ product price} + \$120 \text{ servicing price}} \times \$320 \text{ bundled price} = \$103.78$$

Based on these calculations, Peach can recognize $216.22 of revenue every time it sells the bundled Nectarine support package. However, because Peach must provide one year of service under the support package, the remaining $103.78 of revenue associated with the servicing contract can only be incrementally recognized on a monthly basis over the 12-month life of the service contract, which is $8.65 per month.

MULTIPLE DELIVERABLE DISCLOSURES

The financial statements of a vendor are to include the following disclosures, when applicable:

1. The nature of the vendor's MDAs including provisions relative to performance, cancellation, termination, or refund.
2. The vendor's accounting policy with respect to the recognition of revenue from MDAs (e.g., whether deliverables are separable into units of accounting).

An example of this disclosure requirement follows:

> The company enters into multiple-element revenue arrangements, which may include any combination of services, software, hardware and/or financing. A multiple-element arrangement is separated into more than one unit of accounting if all of the following criteria are met: (1) the delivered item has value to the client on a stand-alone basis; (2) there is objective and reliable evidence of the fair value of the undelivered item; and (3) if the arrangement includes a right of return relative to the delivered item, delivery is considered probable and is under the company's control. If these criteria are met for each element and there is objective and reliable evidence of fair value for all units of accounting in an arrangement, the arrangement consideration is allocated to the separate units of accounting based on each unit's relative fair value. There may be cases, however, in which there is objective and reliable evidence of fair value of the undelivered item but no such evidence for the delivered item. In those cases, the residual method is used to allocate the arrangement consideration. Under the residual method, the amount of consideration allocated to the delivered item equals the total arrangement consideration less the aggregate fair value of the undelivered item. The revenue policies described below are then applied to each unit of accounting, as applicable. If the allocation of consideration in a profitable arrangement results in a loss on an element, that loss is recognized at the earlier of (1) delivery of that element, (2) when the first dollar of revenue is recognized on that element, or (3) when there are no remaining profitable elements in the arrangement to be delivered.

MULTIPLE DELIVERABLE CONTROLS

A company can circumvent these rules by issuing separate contracts for each element of a sale that would normally be considered to have multiple deliverables. One way to spot this issue is to conduct a periodic audit that searches for clusters of contracts entered into with a single customer within a short period of time. The audit program should include a review of these contracts to determine if they are in fact associated with a single sale transaction.

If a company has multiple sale arrangements that include multiple deliverables, it is possible that it will not separate the various elements into separate units of accounting in a consistent manner. To guard against this issue, a periodic audit should compare the documentation of the various MDAs to locate any inconsistencies in the definition of units of accounting.

Another control problem arises when a company records a combination of revenue and "costs and estimated earnings in excess of billings" that exceed the total amount to which a customer has agreed to pay. A billing procedure should require the accounting staff to compare the combination of billings and unbilled costs to the customer's contractual agreement to pay, and record a loss for any costs incurred that exceed this amount.

6 REVENUE RECOGNITION IN FRANCHISING

OVERVIEW

Franchising is a popular growth industry, with many businesses seeking to sell franchises as their primary income source and individuals seeking to buy franchises and become entrepreneurs. Prime accounting issues are how to recognize revenue on the individual sale of franchise territories and on the transactions that arise in connection with the continuing relationship between the franchisor and franchisee.

DEFINITIONS OF TERMS

Area franchise. An agreement that transfers franchise rights within a geographical area, permitting the opening of a number of franchised outlets. The number of outlets, specific locations, and so forth are decisions usually made by the franchisee.

Bargain purchase. A transaction in which the franchisee is allowed to purchase equipment or supplies for a price that is significantly lower than their fair value.

Continuing franchise fee. Consideration for the continuing rights granted by the franchise agreement and for general or specific services during its term.

Franchise agreement. A written business agreement that meets the following principal criteria:

1. The relationship between the franchisor and franchisee is contractual, and an agreement, confirming the rights and responsibilities of each party, is in force for a specified period.
2. The continuing relationship has as its purpose the distribution of a product or service, or an entire business concept, within a particular market area.
3. Both the franchisor and the franchisee contribute resources for establishing and maintaining the franchise. The franchisor's contribution may be a trademark, a company reputation, products, procedures, labor, equipment, or a process. The franchisee usually

contributes operating capital as well as the managerial and operational resources required for opening and continuing the franchised outlet.

4. The franchise agreement outlines and describes the specific marketing practices to be followed, specifies the contribution of each party to the operation of the business, and sets forth certain operating procedures with which both parties agree to comply.

5. The establishment of the franchised outlet creates a business entity that will, in most cases, require and support the full-time business activity of the franchisee.

6. Both the franchisee and the franchisor have a common public identity. This identity is achieved most often through the use of common trade names or trademarks and is frequently reinforced through advertising programs designed to promote the recognition and acceptance of the common identity within the franchisee's market area.

Franchisee. The party who has been granted business rights (the franchise) to operate the franchised business.

Franchisor. The party who grants business rights (the franchise) to the party (the franchisee) who will operate the franchised business.

Initial franchise fee. Consideration for establishing the franchise relationship and providing some agreed-upon initial services. Occasionally, the fee includes consideration for initially required equipment and inventory, but those items usually are the subject of separate consideration. The payment of an initial franchise fee or a continuing royalty fee is not a necessary criterion for an agreement to be considered a franchise agreement.

Initial services. Common provision of a franchise agreement in which the franchisor usually will agree to provide a variety of services and advice to the franchisee, such as the following:

1. Assistance in the selection of a site. The assistance may be based on experience with factors such as traffic patterns, residential configurations, and competition.

2. Assistance in obtaining facilities, including related financing and architectural and engineering services. The facilities may be purchased or leased by the franchisee, and lease payments may be guaranteed by the franchisor.

3. Assistance in advertising, either for the individual franchisee or as part of a general program.

4. Training of the franchisee's personnel.

5. Preparation and distribution of manuals and similar material concerning operations, administration, and recordkeeping.
6. Bookkeeping and advisory services, including setting up the franchisee's records and advising the franchisee about income taxes, real estate taxes, and other taxes, or about local regulations affecting the franchisee's business.
7. Inspection, testing, and other quality control programs.

FRANCHISE SALES

Franchise operations are generally subject to the same accounting principles as other commercial enterprises. Special issues arise out of franchise agreements, however, which require the application of special accounting rules.

Revenue is recognized, with an appropriate provision for bad debts, when the franchisor has substantially performed all material services or conditions. Only when revenue is collected over an extended period of time and collectibility cannot be predicted in advance would the use of the cost recovery or installment methods of revenue recognition be appropriate. "Substantial performance" means

1. The franchisor has no remaining obligation to either refund cash or forgive any unpaid balance due.
2. Substantially all initial services required by the agreement have been performed.
3. No material obligations or conditions remain.

Even if the contract does not require initial services, the pattern of performance by the franchisor in other franchise sales will impact the time period of revenue recognition. This can delay such recognition until either services are performed or it can be reasonably assured they will not be performed. The franchisee operations will be considered as started when such substantial performance has occurred.

If initial franchise fees are large compared to services rendered and continuing franchise fees are small compared to services to be rendered, then a portion of the initial fee is deferred in an amount sufficient to cover the costs of future services plus a reasonable profit, after considering the impact of the continuing franchise fee.

Example of initial franchise fee revenue recognition

Shanghai Oriental Cuisine sells a Quack's Roast Duck franchise to Toledo Restaurants. The franchise is renewable after two years. The initial franchise fee is $50,000, plus a fixed fee of $500 per month. In exchange, Shanghai provides staff training, vendor relations support, and site selection consulting. Each month thereafter, Shanghai provides $1,000 of free local advertising. Shanghai's typical gross margin on franchise start-up sales is 25%.

Because the monthly fee does not cover the cost of monthly services provided, Shanghai defers a portion of the initial franchise fee and amortizes it over the two-year life of the franchise agreement, using the following calculation:

	Cost of monthly services provided $1,000 × 24 months	=	$24,000
÷	Markup to equal standard 25% gross margin	=	.75
=	Estimated revenue required to offset monthly services provided	=	$32,000
	Less: Monthly billing to franchise $500 × 24 months	=	$12,000
=	Amount of initial franchise fee to be deferred	=	$20,000

Shanghai's entry to record the franchise fee deferral follows:

Franchise fee revenue	20,000	
Unearned franchise fees (liability)		20,000

Shanghai recognizes 1/24 of the unearned franchise fee liability during each month of the franchise period on a straight-line basis, which amounts to $833.33 per month.

AREA FRANCHISE SALES

Sometimes franchisors sell territories rather than individual locations. In this event, the franchisor may render services to the area independent of the number of individual franchises to be established. Under this circumstance, revenue recognition for the franchisor is the same as stated above. If, however, substantial services are performed by the franchisor for each individual franchise established, then revenue is recognized in proportion to the amount of mandatory service. The general rule is that when the franchisee has no right to receive a refund, all revenue is recognized. It may be necessary for revenue recognition purposes to treat a franchise agreement as a divisible contract and allocate revenue among existing and estimated locations. Future revisions to these estimates will require that remaining unrecognized revenue be recorded in proportion to remaining services expected to be performed.

Example of revenue recognition for area franchise sales

Shanghai Oriental Cuisine sells an area Quack's Roast Duck franchise to Canton Investments for $40,000. Under the terms of this area franchise, Shanghai is solely obligated to provide site selection consulting services to every franchise that Canton opens during the next 12 months, after which Canton is not entitled to a refund. Canton estimates that it will open 12 outlets sporadically throughout the year. Shanghai estimates that it will cost $2,500 for each site selection, or $30,000 in total. Based on the initial

$40,000 franchise fee, Shanghai's estimated gross margin is 25 percent. Canton's initial payment of $40,000 is recorded by Shanghai with the following entry:

Cash	40,000	
Unearned franchise fees (liability)		40,000

After six months of preparation, Canton requests that four site selection surveys be completed. Shanghai completes the work at a cost of $10,000 and uses the following entry to record both the expenditure and related revenue:

Unearned franchise fees (liability)	13,333	
Franchise fee revenue		13,333
Site survey expense	10,000	
Accounts payable		10,000

By the end of the year, Shanghai has performed 10 site selection surveys at a cost of $25,000 and recognized revenue of $33,333, leaving $6,667 of unrecognized revenue. Since Canton is no longer entitled to a refund, Shanghai uses the following entry to recognize all remaining revenue, with no related expense:

Unearned franchise fees (liability)	6,667	
Franchise fee revenue		6,667

OTHER RELATIONSHIPS

Franchisors may guarantee debt of the franchisee, continue to own a portion of the franchise, or control the franchisee's operations. Revenue is not recognized until all services, conditions, and obligations have been performed.

In addition, the franchisor may have an option to reacquire the location. Accounting for initial revenue is to consider the probability of exercise of the option. If the expectation at the time of the agreement is that the option is likely to be exercised, the entire franchise fee is deferred and not recognized as income. Upon exercise, the deferral reduces the recorded investment of the franchisor.

An initial fee may cover both franchise rights and property rights, including equipment, signs, and inventory. A portion of the fee applicable to property rights is recognized to the extent of the fair value of these assets. However, fees relating to different services rendered by franchisors are generally not allocated to these different services because segregating the amounts applicable to each service could not be performed objectively. The rule of revenue recognition when all services are substantially performed is generally upheld. If objectively determinable separate fees are charged for separate services, then recognition of revenue can be determined and recorded for each service performed.

Franchisors may act as agents for the franchisee by issuing purchase orders to suppliers for inventory and equipment. These are not recorded as sales and purchases by the franchisor; instead, consistent with the agency relationship, receivables from the franchisee and payables to the supplier are reported on the balance sheet of the franchisor. There is, of course, no right of offset associated with these amounts, which are to be presented gross.

CONTINUING FRANCHISE AND OTHER FEES

Continuing franchise fees are recognized as revenue as the fees are earned. Related costs are expensed as incurred. Regardless of the purpose of the fees, revenue is recognized when the fee is earned and receivable. The exception is when a portion of the fee is required to be segregated and used for a specific purpose, such as advertising. The franchisor defers this amount and records it as a liability. This liability is reduced by the cost of the services received.

Sometimes the franchisee has a period of time in which bargain purchases of equipment or supplies are granted by the contract. If the bargain price is lower than other customers pay or denies a reasonable profit to the franchisor, a portion of the initial franchise fee is deferred and accounted for as an adjustment of the selling price when the franchisee makes the purchase. The deferred amount is either the difference in the selling price among customers and the bargain price, or an amount sufficient to provide a reasonable profit to the franchisor.

COSTS

Direct and incremental costs related to franchise sales are deferred and recognized when revenue is recorded. However, deferred costs cannot exceed anticipated future revenue, net of additional expected costs.

Indirect costs are expensed as incurred. These usually are regular and recurring costs that bear no relationship to sales.

REPOSSESSED FRANCHISES

If, for any reason, the franchisor refunds the franchise fee and obtains the location, previously recognized revenue is reversed in the period of repossession. If a repossession is made without a refund, there is no adjustment of revenue previously recognized. However, any estimated uncollectible amounts are to be provided for, and any remaining collected funds are recorded as revenue.

BUSINESS COMBINATIONS

In business combinations where the franchisor acquires the business of a franchisee, no adjustment of prior revenue is made, since the financial statements are not retroactively consolidated in recording a business combination. Care must be taken to ensure that the purchase is not a repossession. If the transaction is deemed to be a repossession, it is accounted for as described in the preceding section.

DISCLOSURE OF FRANCHISING REVENUE RECOGNITION

There are several disclosures required for franchise fee transactions. They include

- The types of significant commitments resulting from franchising arrangements, as well as franchisor services not yet performed.
- The franchise sale price.
- The amount of deferred revenue and costs.
- The periods when fees become payable by the franchisee.
- The amounts of revenue initially deferred due to collectibility uncertainties, but then recognized due to resolution of the uncertainties.
- The number of franchises sold, purchased, and in operation during the period (which shall segregate the number of franchisor-owned outlets in operation from the number of franchisee-owned operations).
- Segregate the reporting of initial franchise fees from other franchise fee revenue, if they are significant.
- Segregate the revenues and costs of franchisor-owned outlets from those of franchisees, when practicable.
- If there is no reasonable basis for estimating the ability of the franchisor to collect franchise fees, the type of accounting method used to recognize franchise fee revenue (either the installment or cost recovery method) must be disclosed.
- If initial franchise fee revenue is likely to decline because of market saturation, this issue should be disclosed.

Here are several examples of company disclosures that follow some of the preceding reporting requirements:

1. The Company's revenues consist of sales by Company-operated restaurants and fees from restaurants operated by franchisees and affiliates. Sales by Company-operated restaurants are recognized on a cash basis. Fees from franchised and affiliated restaurants include continuing rent and service fees, initial fees, and royalties received from foreign affiliates and developmental licensees. Continuing fees and royalties are recog-

nized in the period earned. Initial fees are recognized upon opening of a restaurant, which is when the Company has performed substantially all initial services required by the franchise arrangement.

2. The Company enters into franchise agreements committing to provide franchisees with various marketing services and limited rights to utilize the Company's registered trademarks. These agreements typically have an initial term of 10 years, with provisions permitting franchisees to terminate after 5 years under certain circumstances. In most instances, initial franchise fees are recognized upon execution of the franchise agreement because the initial franchise fee is nonrefundable and the Company has no continuing obligations related to the franchisee. The initial franchise fee related to executed franchise agreements, which include incentives such as future potential rebates, are deferred and recognized when the incentive criteria are met or the agreement is terminated, whichever occurs first.

3. The following are changes in the Company's franchised locations for each of the fiscal years 2008 through 2010:

	2010	2009	2008
Franchises in operation—beginning of year	7,958	7,637	7,322
Franchises opened	355	425	470
Franchises closed	(121)	(122)	(104)
Net transfers within the system	(1)	18	(51)
Franchises in operation—end of year	8,191	7,958	7,637
Company-owned stores	1,758	1,748	1,672
Total system-wide stores	9,949	9,706	9,309

FRANCHISING REVENUE POLICIES AND PROCEDURES

It is possible for the franchisor to front-end load an excessive amount of its fees into the initial franchise fee rather than into its continuing royalty agreement, thereby falsely accelerating revenue recognition. To avoid this, an accounting policy can state that the initial and continuing fees shall be periodically examined and changed to ensure that each one had approximately the same estimated gross margin.

Another accounting policy should state that the initial franchise fee shall not be recognized until all start-up services to be provided by the franchisor have been completed. This policy keeps the accounting staff from recognizing revenue too early.

Under an area franchise sale agreement, the franchisor typically recognizes initial fee revenue based on the proportion of actual franchise locations completed within the area as a proportion of the total estimated number to be completed. Since the amount of revenue recognized is driven by the estimated number of total franchise locations in the area, an accounting policy should state that this estimate be regularly reviewed and updated as necessary.

If deferred costs related to a franchise exceed the amount of the franchise fee, then the excess costs must be recognized at once. An accounting policy should state that this comparison be made as part of the month-end closing procedure.

FRANCHISING REVENUE CONTROLS

To ensure that revenue recognition is not accelerated through the use of an excessively high initial franchise fee in proportion to services generated, a periodic audit could calculate and compare the gross margins earned on initial and ongoing franchise fees. It is also possible that revenue could be recognized on an initial franchise fee before all related services have been completed, thereby falsely accelerating revenue recognition. To detect this problem, a periodic audit could compare the completion of services to the recognition of initial franchise fee revenue for each franchise agreement.

It is possible to incorrectly accelerate the recognition of initial franchise fees when area franchise sales have been made, simply by underestimating the number of franchise locations to be situated within the area franchise. A periodic audit can investigate the number of actual and estimated franchise locations used in the revenue recognition calculation to determine if improperly low estimates have been used.

The franchisor may recognize ongoing franchise fees automatically, without regard to whether related services have been provided at the same time. This is most likely to occur when certain activities, such as advertising campaigns, are conducted only at long intervals, and therefore do not coincide with the receipt of franchisee payments. As a result, revenue is incorrectly recognized prior to the completion of all related services by the franchisor. To detect this issue, a periodic audit should review the calculations used to recognize ongoing franchise revenue, and whether some revenue recognition is withheld pending the completion of such services.

7 REVENUE RECOGNITION FOR LONG-TERM CONSTRUCTION CONTRACTS

OVERVIEW

Accounting for long-term construction contracts involves questions as to when revenue is to be recognized and how to measure the revenue to be recorded.

Long-term construction contract revenue is recognizable over time as construction progresses rather than at the completion of the contract. This "as earned" approach to revenue recognition is justified because under most long-term construction contracts both the buyer and the seller (contractor) obtain legally enforceable rights. The buyer has the legal right to require specific performance from the contractor and, in effect, has an ownership claim to the contractor's work-in-progress. The contractor, under most long-term contracts, has the right to require the buyer to make progress payments during the construction period. The substance of this business activity is that revenue is earned continuously as the work progresses.

DEFINITIONS OF TERMS

Back charges. Billings for work performed or costs incurred by one party (the biller) that, in accordance with the agreement, should have been performed or incurred by the party billed.

Change order. A legal document executed by a contractor and customer (which can be initiated by either) that modifies selected terms of a contract (e.g., pricing, timing and scope of work) without the necessity of redrafting the entire contract.

Claims. Amounts in excess of the agreed contract price that a contractor seeks to collect from customers for customer-caused delays, errors in specifications and designs, unapproved change orders, or other causes of unanticipated costs.

Combining contracts. Grouping two or more contracts into a single profit center for accounting purposes.

Completed-contract method. A method of accounting that recognizes revenue only after the contract is complete.

Cost-to-cost method. A percentage-of-completion method used to determine the extent of progress toward completion on a contract. The ratio of costs incurred from project inception through the end of the current period (numerator) to the total estimated costs of the project (denominator) is applied to the contract price (as adjusted for change orders) to determine total contract revenue earned to date.

Estimated cost to complete. The anticipated additional cost of materials, labor, subcontracting costs, and indirect costs (overhead) required to complete a project at a scheduled time.

Percentage-of-completion method. A method of accounting that recognizes revenue on a contract as work progresses.

Precontract costs. Costs incurred before a contract has been accepted (e.g., architectural designs, purchase of special equipment, engineering fees, and start-up costs).

Profit center. A unit for the accumulation of revenues and costs for the measurement of contract performance.

Progress billings on long-term contracts. Requests for partial payments sent to the customer in accordance with the terms of the contract at agreed-upon intervals as various project milestones are reached.

Segmenting contracts. Dividing a single contract or group of contracts into two or more profit centers for accounting purposes.

Subcontractor. A second-level contractor who enters into a contract with a prime (general) contractor to perform a specific part or phase of a construction project.

Substantial completion. The point at which the major work on a contract is completed and only insignificant costs and potential risks remain.

Work-in-progress (WIP). The accumulated construction costs of the project that have been incurred since project inception.

THE PERCENTAGE-OF-COMPLETION METHOD

These are two generally accepted methods of accounting for long-term construction contracts. One of these methods is the *percentage-of-completion method,* which recognizes income as work on a contract (or group of closely related contracts) progresses. The recognition of revenues and profits is generally related to costs incurred in providing the services required under the contract.

Under this method, WIP is accumulated in the accounting records. At any point in time if the cumulative billings to date under the contract exceed the amount of the WIP plus the portion of the contract's estimated gross profit attributable to that WIP, then the contractor recognizes a current liability captioned "billings in excess of costs and estimated earnings." This liability recognizes the remaining obligation of the contractor to complete additional work prior to recognizing the excess billing as revenue.

If the reverse is true, that is, the accumulated WIP and gross profit earned exceed billings to date, then the contractor recognizes a current asset captioned "costs and estimated earnings in excess of billings." This asset represents the portion of the contractor's revenues under the contract that have been earned but not yet billed under the contract provisions. Where more than one contract exists, these assets and liabilities are determined on a project-by-project basis, with the accumulated assets and liabilities being separately stated on the balance sheet. Assets and liabilities are not offset unless a right of offset exists. Thus, the net debit balances for certain contracts are not ordinarily offset against net credit balances for other contracts.

Under the percentage-of-completion method, income is not based on cash collections or interim billings. Cash collections and interim billings are based on contract terms that do not necessarily measure contract performance.

THE COMPLETED-CONTRACT METHOD

The *completed-contract method* recognizes income only when the contract is complete, or substantially complete. Under this method, contract costs and related billings are accumulated in the accounting records and reported as deferred items on the balance sheet until the project is complete or substantially complete. A contract is regarded as substantially complete if remaining costs of completion are immaterial. When the accumulated costs (WIP) exceed the related billings, the excess is presented as a current asset (inventory account). If billings exceed related costs, the difference is presented as a current liability. This determination is also made on a project-by-project basis with the accumulated assets and liabilities being separately stated on the balance sheet. An excess of accumulated costs over related billings is presented as a current asset, and an excess of accumulated billings over related costs is presented in most cases as a current liability.

Preferability Assessment

The percentage-of-completion method is preferable when estimates are reasonably dependable and the following conditions exist:

1. Contracts executed by the parties include provisions that clearly specify the enforceable rights regarding goods or services to be provided and received by the parties, the consideration to be exchanged, and the manner and terms of settlement.
2. The buyer can be expected to satisfy his or her obligations under the contract.
3. The contractor can be expected to perform his or her contractual obligations.

This scenario presumes that contractors generally have the ability to produce estimates that are sufficiently dependable to justify the use of the percentage-of-completion method of accounting. Persuasive evidence to the contrary is necessary to overcome this presumption.

The principal advantage of the completed-contract method is that it is based on final results, whereas the percentage-of-completion method is dependent on estimates for unperformed work. The principal disadvantage of the completed-contract method is that when the period of a contract extends into more than one accounting period, there will be an irregular recognition of income.

These two methods are not to be used as acceptable alternatives for the same set of circumstances. In general, when estimates of costs to complete and extent of progress toward completion of long-term contracts are reasonably dependable, the percentage-of-completion method is preferable. When lack of dependable estimates or inherent hazards cause forecasts to be doubtful, the completed-contract method is preferable.

The completed-contract method may also be acceptable when a contractor has numerous relatively short-term contracts and when results of operations do not vary materially from those that would be reported under the percentage-of-completion method.

Based on the contractor's individual circumstances, a decision is made as to whether to apply completed-contract or percentage-of-completion accounting as the entity's basic accounting policy. If warranted by different facts and circumstances regarding a particular contract or group of contracts, that contract or group of contracts is to be accounted for under the other method with accompanying financial statement disclosures of this departure from the normal policy.

Costs Incurred

Precontract costs are costs incurred before a contract has been entered into, with the expectation of the contract being accepted and thereby recoverable through future billings. Precontract costs include architectural designs, costs of learning a new process, and any other costs that are expected to be recovered if the contract is accepted. Precontract costs should be expensed as incurred, as they are the equivalent of start-up costs in other types of businesses. Consequently, precontract costs are not permitted to be included in WIP. Contract costs incurred after the acceptance of the contract are costs incurred toward the completion of the project and are accumulated in WIP.

If precontract costs are incurred in connection with a current contract in anticipation of obtaining additional future contracts, those costs are nevertheless accounted for as costs of the current contract. If such costs are not incurred in connection with a current contract, then they must be expensed as incurred. There is no look-back provision. A contractor may not retroactively record precontract costs as WIP if a contract is subsequently executed.

Contract costs are costs identifiable with or allocable to specific contracts. Generally, contract costs include all direct costs, such as direct materials, direct labor, and any indirect costs (overhead) allocable to the contracts. Contract costs can be broken down into two categories: costs incurred to date and estimated costs to complete.

The company may choose to defer costs related to producing excess goods in anticipation of future orders of the same item. Costs associated with excess production can be treated as inventory if the costs are considered recoverable.

Estimated costs to complete are the anticipated costs required to complete a project at a scheduled time. They are comprised of the same elements as the original total estimated contract costs and are based on prices expected to be in effect when the costs will be incurred. The latest estimates are used to determine the progress toward completion.

Systematic and consistent procedures are to be used. These procedures are to be correlated with the cost accounting system in order to facilitate a comparison between actual and estimated costs. Additionally, the determination of estimated total contract costs is to identify the significant cost elements.

Estimated costs are to reflect any expected price increases. These expected price increases are not "blanket provisions" for all contract costs, but rather specific provisions for each specific type of cost. Expected increases in each of the cost elements such as wages, materials, and overhead items are considered separately.

Finally, estimates of costs to complete are to be reviewed periodically to reflect new information. Estimates of costs are to be examined for price fluctuations and reviewed for possible future problems, such as labor strikes or direct material delivery delays.

Accounting for contract costs is similar to accounting for inventory. Costs necessary to ready the asset for sale (transfer of possession and occupancy by the customer) are recorded in WIP as incurred. WIP includes both direct and indirect costs but not general and administrative expenses or selling expenses since, by definition, they are not identifiable with a particular contract and are therefore treated as period costs. However, general and administrative expenses may be included in contract costs under the completed-contract method since this could result in better matching of revenues and costs, especially in years when no contracts were completed.

Since a contractor may not be able to perform all facets of a construction project, one or more subcontractors may be engaged. *Subcontractor costs* are included in contract costs as the work is completed. These amounts are directly attributable to the project and included in WIP, similar to direct materials and direct labor.

Contract costs may require adjustment for back charges. A *back charge* is a billing by the contractor to a subcontractor (or a reduction in the amount due to that subcontractor under the subcontract) for costs incurred by the contractor to complete or correct work that the contract stipulated was to have been performed by the subcontractor. These charges are often disputed by the parties involved.

Example of a back charge situation

The subcontract (the contract between the general contractor and the subcontractor) obligates the subcontractor to raze a building and prepare the land for construction of a replacement building. The general contractor had to clear away debris left by the subcontractor before construction could begin. The general contractor expects to be reimbursed for the work since it was required to be performed by the subcontractor. The contractor back charges the subcontractor for the costs of debris removal.

The contractor treats the back charge as a receivable from the subcontractor (or a reduction in the amount payable to the subcontractor) and reduces contract costs by the amount recoverable. If the subcontractor disputes the back charge, the cost becomes a claim. Claims are an amount in excess of the agreed contract price or amounts not included in the original contract price that the contractor seeks to collect.

The subcontractor records the back charge as a payable and as additional contract costs if it is probable the amount will be paid. If the amount or validity of the liability is disputed, the subcontractor considers the probable outcome in order to determine the proper accounting treatment.

Types of Contracts

Four types of contracts are distinguished based on their pricing arrangements: (1) fixed-price or lump-sum contracts, (2) time-and-materials contracts, (3) cost-type contracts, and (4) unit-price contracts.

Fixed-price contracts are contracts for which the price is not usually subject to adjustment because of costs incurred by the contractor. The contractor bears the risks of cost overruns.

Time-and-materials contracts are contracts that provide for payments to the contractor based on direct labor hours at fixed rates and the contractor's cost of materials.

Cost-type contracts provide for reimbursement of allowable or otherwise defined costs incurred plus a fee representing profits. Some variations of cost-plus contracts are

1. Cost-without-fee: no provision for a fee
2. Cost-plus-fixed-fee: contractor reimbursed for costs plus provision for a fixed fee
3. Cost-plus-award-fee: same as cost-plus-fixed-fee plus a provision for an award based on performance

The contract price on a cost-type contract is determined by the sum of the reimbursable expenditures and a fee. The fee is the profit margin (revenue less direct expenses) to be earned on the contract.

Unit-price contracts are contracts under which the contractor is paid a specified amount for every unit of work performed.

Contract costs (incurred and estimated to complete) are used to compute the gross profit or loss recognized. Under the percentage-of-completion method, gross profit or loss is recognized in each period. The revenue recognized is matched against the contract costs incurred (similar to cost of goods sold) to determine gross profit or loss. Under the completed-contract method, the gross profit or loss is determined at the substantial completion of the contract, and no revenue or contract costs are recognized until this point.

Additionally, inventoriable costs (accumulated in WIP) are never to exceed the net realizable value (NRV) of the contract. When contract costs exceed their NRV, they must be written down, requiring a contract loss to be recognized in the current period (this will be discussed in greater detail later). This is similar to accounting for inventory.

Example of contract types

Domino Construction, Inc. enters into a government contract to construct an early-warning radar dome. The contract amount is for $1,900,000, on which Domino expects to incur costs of $1,750,000 and earn a profit of $150,000. Costs expected to be incurred on the project are

Concrete pad	175,000
Pad installation labor	100,000
Radar dome	1,150,000
Dome installation labor	325,000
Total cost	1,750,000

This is a two-month project, where a concrete pad is installed during the first month and a prefabricated dome is assembled on the pad during the second month. To comply with bank loan agreements, complete GAAP-basis financial statements are prepared by Domino at each month-end. Domino encounters problems pouring the concrete pad, requiring its removal and reinstallation. The extra cost incurred is $175,000. During the second month, in order to meet the completion deadline, Domino spends an extra $35,000 on overtime for the dome construction crew. Domino records different billable amounts and profits under the following five contract scenarios:

1. *Fixed-price contract.* At the end of the first month of work, Domino has already lost all of its profit and expects to incur an additional loss of $25,000. It then incurs an additional loss of $35,000 in the second month. Domino issues one billing upon completion of the project. Its calculation of losses on the contract follows:

	Month 1	Month 2
Total billing at completion	1,900,000	1,900,000
− Expected total costs	(1,750,000)	(1,925,000)
− Additional costs	(175,000)	(35,000)
+ Loss already recorded	—	25,000
= Loss to record in current period	(25,000)	(35,000)

2. *Cost-plus-fixed fee.* Domino completes the same project, but bills it to the government at cost at the end of each month, as well as a $150,000 fixed fee at the end of the project that is essentially a project management fee and which comprises all of Domino's profit. The project completion entry follows:

	Month 1	Month 2	Totals
Expected material costs	175,000	1,150,000	1,325,000
+ Additional material costs	175,000	—	175,000
+ Expected labor costs	100,000	325,000	425,000
+ Additional labor costs	—	35,000	35,000
+ Fixed fee	—	150,000	150,000
= Total billing	450,000	1,660,000	2,110,000

3. *Cost-plus-award.* Domino completes the same cost-plus-fixed-fee contract just described, but also bills the government an additional $50,000 for achieving the stipulated construction deadline, resulting in a total profit of $200,000. The project completion entry follows:

	Month 1	*Month 2*	*Totals*
Expected material costs	175,000	1,150,000	1,325,000
+ Additional material costs	175,000	—	175,000
+ Expected labor costs	100,000	325,000	425,000
+ Additional labor costs	—	35,000	35,000
+ Fixed fee	—	150,000	150,000
+ Timely completion bonus	—	50,000	50,000
= Total billing	450,000	1,710,000	2,160,000

4. *Time-and-materials contract with no spending cap.* Domino completes the same project, but bills all costs incurred at the end of each month to the government. The additional material cost of the concrete pad is billed at cost, while the overtime incurred is billed at a standard hourly rate with a 25% markup. Domino's profit is contained within the markup on its labor billings. Domino records a profit on the project of $115,000 on total billings of $2,075,000. Its calculation of profits on the contract follows:

	Month 1	*Month 2*	*Totals*
Expected material costs	175,000	1,150,000	1,325,000
+ Additional material costs	175,000	—	175,000
+ Expected labor costs	100,000	325,000	425,000
+ Additional labor costs	—	35,000	35,000
+ 25% profit on labor costs billed	25,000	90,000	115,000
= Total billing	475,000	1,600,000	2,075,000

5. *Time-and-materials contract with spending cap.* Domino completes the same time-and-materials project just described, but the contract authorization is divided into two task orders; one authorizes a spending cap of $450,000 on the concrete pad installation, while the second task order caps spending on the radar dome at $1,500,000. Domino records a loss of $10,000 on total billings of $1,950,000. Its calculation of profits on the contract follows:

	Month 1	*Month 2*	*Totals*
Expected material costs	175,000	1,150,000	1,325,000
+ Additional material costs	175,000	—	175,000
+ Expected labor costs	100,000	325,000	425,000
+ Additional labor costs	—	35,000	35,000
+ 25% profit on labor costs billed	25,000	90,000	115,000
– Spending cap limitation	(25,000)	(100,000)	(125,000)
= Total billing	450,000	1,500,000	1,950,000

REVENUE MEASUREMENT

In practice, various methods are used to measure the extent of progress toward completion. The most common methods are the cost-to-cost method, efforts-expended method, units-of-delivery method, and units-of-work-performed method. Each of these methods of measuring progress on a contract can be identified as either an input or output measure.

The input measures attempt to identify progress on a contract in terms of the efforts devoted to it. The cost-to-cost and efforts-expended methods are examples of input measures. Under the cost-to-cost method, the percentage of completion is estimated by comparing total costs incurred from the inception of the job to date (numerator) to total costs expected for the entire job (denominator).

Output measures are made in terms of results by attempting to identify progress toward completion by physical measures. The units-of-delivery and units-of-work-performed methods are examples of output measures. Under both of these methods, an estimate of completion is made in terms of achievements to date.

Both input and output measures have drawbacks in certain circumstances. A significant problem of input measures is that the relationship between input and productivity is only indirect; inefficiencies and other factors can cause this relationship to change. A particular drawback of the cost-to-cost method is that costs of uninstalled materials and other up-front costs may produce higher estimates of the percentage-of-completion because of their early incurrence. These costs are excluded from the cost-to-cost computation or allocated over the contract life when it appears that a better measure of contract progress will be obtained.

A significant problem of output measures is that the cost, time, and effort associated with one unit of output may not be comparable to that of another. For example, because of the cost of the foundation, the costs to complete the first story of a 20-story office building can be expected to be greater than the costs of the remaining 19 floors.

The cost-to-cost method has become one of the most popular measures used to determine the extent of progress toward completion. Under the cost-to-cost method, the percentage of revenue to recognize can be determined by the following formula:

$$\left(\frac{\text{Cost to date}}{\text{Cost to date} + \text{Estimated costs to complete}} \times \text{Contract price} \right) - \text{Revenue previously recognized} = \text{Current revenue recognized}$$

By slightly modifying this formula, current gross profit can also be determined.

$$\left(\frac{\text{Cost to date}}{\text{Cost to date} + \text{Estimated costs to complete}} \times \text{Expected total gross profit} \right) - \text{Gross profit previously recognized} = \text{Current gross profit earned}$$

Example of percentage-of-completion (cost-to-cost) and completed-contract methods with a profitable contract

Assume a $500,000 contract that requires three years to complete and incurs a total cost of $405,000. The following data pertain to the construction period:

	Year 1	Year 2	Year 3
Costs incurred during the period	$150,000	$210,000	$ 45,000
Cumulative costs incurred to date	150,000	360,000	405,000
Estimated costs yet to be incurred at year-end	300,000	40,000	—
Estimated total costs	450,000	400,000	—
Progress billings made during the year	100,000	370,000	30,000
Cumulative billings to date	100,000	470,000	500,000
Collections of billings	75,000	300,000	125,000

Journal Entries Common to Completed-Contract and Percentage-of-Completion Methods

	Year 1		Year 2		Year 3	
Work-in-progress	150,000		210,000		45,000	
Cash, payables, etc.		150,000		210,000		45,000
Contract receivables	100,000		370,000		30,000	
Billings on contracts		100,000		370,000		30,000
Cash	75,000		300,000		125,000	
Contract receivables		75,000		300,000		125,000

Journal Entries for Completed-Contract Method Only

Billings on contracts		500,000		
Cost of revenues earned		405,000		
Contract revenues earned				500,000
Work-in-progress				405,000

Journal Entries for Percentage-of-Completion Method Only

	Year 1		Year 2		Year 3	
Cost of revenues earned	150,000		210,000		45,000	
Work-in-progress		150,000		210,000		45,000
Billings on contracts	100,000		370,000		30,000	
Contract revenues earned		166,667		283,333		50,000
Costs and estimated earnings in excess of billings on uncompleted contracts	66,667		66,667			
Billings in excess of costs and estimated earnings on uncompleted contracts			20,000	20,000		

Income Statement Presentation

	Year 1	Year 2	Year 3	Total
Percentage-of-completion				
Contract revenues earned	$166,667[a]	$283,333[b]	$ 50,000[c]	$ 500,000
Cost of revenues earned	(150,000)	(210,000)	(45,000)	(405,000)
Gross profit	$ 16,667	$ 73,333	$ 5,000	$ 95,000
Completed-contract				
Contract revenues earned	—	—	$ 500,000	$ 500,000
Cost of revenues completed	—	—	(405,000)	(405,000)
Gross profit	—	—	$ 95,000	$ 95,000

* $\dfrac{\$150,000}{450,000} \times 500,000 = \$166,667$

** $\left(\dfrac{\$360,000}{400,000} \times 500,000\right) - \$166,667 = \$283,333$

*** $\left(\dfrac{\$405,000}{405,000} \times 500,000\right) - \$166,667 - 283,333 = \$50,000$

Balance Sheet Presentation

	Year 1	Year 2	Year 3
Percentage-of-completion			
Current assets:			
Contract receivables	$25,000	$95,000	[a]
Costs and estimated earnings in excess of billings on uncompleted contracts	66,667		
Current liabilities:			
Billings in excess of costs and estimated earnings on uncompleted contracts, year 2		20,000	
Completed-contract			
Current assets:			
Contract receivables	$25,000	$ 95,000	[a]
Costs in excess of billings on uncompleted contracts			
Work-in-progress	150,000		
Less billings on long-term contracts	(100,000)	$50,000	
Current liabilities:			
Billings in excess of costs on uncompleted contracts, year 2 ($470,000 – 360,000)		$110,000	

[a] *Since the contract was completed, there are no balance sheet amounts at the end of year 3.*

Some contractors adopt an accounting policy of not recognizing any gross profit on a contract that is less than 10% complete. This election is usually made for two reasons:

1. The contractor is qualified to make and has made the election permitted by Internal Revenue Code §460(b)(5) to defer the recogni-

tion of such gross profit for U.S. federal income tax purposes and wishes to avoid computational differences between applying the percentage-of-completion method for financial reporting and tax purposes.

2. The contractor believes that this policy is prudent given the uncertainties associated with a contract that is so close to inception.

The GAAP effect of such a policy is usually immaterial, and the accountant normally need not be concerned about it being a departure from GAAP.

Contract Losses

When the current estimate of total contract costs exceeds the current estimate of total contract revenues, a provision for the entire loss on the entire contract is made. Losses are recognized in the period in which they become evident under either the percentage-of-completion method or the completed-contract method. The loss is computed on the basis of the total estimated costs to complete the contract, including the contract costs incurred to date plus estimated costs (use the same elements as contract costs incurred) to complete. The loss is presented as a separately captioned current liability on the balance sheet.

In any year when a percentage-of-completion contract has an expected loss, the amount of the loss reported in that year is computed as follows:

Reported loss = Total expected loss + All profit previously recognized

Example of percentage-of-completion and completed-contract methods with loss contract

Using the previous information, if the estimated costs yet to be incurred at the end of year two were $148,000, the total expected loss is $8,000 [$500,000 − (360,000 + 148,000)], and the total loss reported in year 2 would be $24,667 ($8,000 + 16,667). Under the completed-contract method, the loss recognized is simply the total expected loss, $8,000.

Journal Entry at End of Year 2	*Percentage-of-completion*	*Completed-contract*
Loss on uncompleted long-term contract (expense)	24,667	8,000
Estimated loss on uncompleted contract (liability)	24,667	8,000

Profit or Loss Recognized on Contract
(Percentage-of-Completion Method)

	Year 1	*Year 2*	*Year 3*
Contract price	$500,000	$500,000	$500,000
Estimated total costs:			
Costs incurred contract-to-date	150,000	360,000	506,000[a]
Estimated costs yet to be incurred	300,000	148,000	—
Estimated total costs for the three-year period, actual for year 3	450,000	508,000	506,000
Estimated gross profit (loss), actual for year 3	50,000	(8,000)	(6,000)
Summary of Effect on Results of Operations			
Current end-of-year estimate of gross profit (loss) actual for year 3	—	$ (8,000)	$ (6,000)
Accumulated effect of gross profit (loss) recognized in prior years	—	16,667	(8,000)
Effect on gross profit (loss) recognized in current year	$ —	$ (24,667)	$ 2,000

   [a] *Assumed*

Profit or Loss Recognized on Contract
(Completed-Contract Method)

	Year 1	*Year 2*	*Year 3*
Contract price	$500,000	$500,000	$500,000
Estimated total costs:			
Costs incurred to date	150,000	360,000	506,000[a]
Estimated cost yet to be incurred	300,000	148,000	—
Estimated total costs for the three-year period, actual for year 3	450,000	508,000	506,000
Estimated profit (loss), inception-to-date, actual for year 3	50,000	(8,000)	(6,000)
Loss previously recognized	—	—	(8,000)
Amount of estimated income (loss) recognized in the current period, actual for year 3	$ —	$ (8,000)	$ 2,000

   [a] *Assumed*

Upon completion of the project during year 3, it can be seen that the actual loss was only $6,000 ($500,000 – $506,000); therefore, the estimated loss provision was overstated in previous years by $2,000. However, since this is a change of an estimate, the $2,000 difference must be handled prospectively; consequently, $2,000 of income is recognized in year 3 ($8,000 loss previously recognized – $6,000 actual loss).

Combining and Segmenting Contracts

The profit center for accounting purposes is usually a single contract, but under some circumstances the profit center may be a combination of two or more contracts, a segment of a contract or a group of combined contracts.

For accounting purposes, a group of contracts may be combined if they are so closely related that they are, in substance, parts of a single project with an overall profit margin. A group of contracts may be combined if the contracts

1. Are negotiated as a package in the same economic environment with an overall profit margin objective.
2. Constitute an agreement to do a single project.
3. Require closely interrelated construction activities.
4. Are performed concurrently or in a continuous sequence under the same project management.
5. Constitute, in substance, an agreement with a single customer.

Segmenting a contract is a process of breaking up a larger unit into smaller units for accounting purposes. If the project is segmented, revenues are assigned to the different elements or phases to achieve different rates of profitability based on the relative value of each element or phase to the estimated total contract revenue. A project may be segmented if all of the following steps were taken and are documented and verifiable:

1. The contractor submitted bona fide proposals on the separate components of the project and on the entire project.
2. The customer had the right to accept the proposals on either basis.
3. The aggregate amount of the proposals on the separate components approximated the amount of the proposal on the entire project.

A project that does not meet the above criteria may still be segmented if all of the following are applicable:

1. The terms and scope of the contract or project clearly call for the separable phases or elements.
2. The separable phases or elements of the project are often bid or negotiated separately in the marketplace.
3. The market assigns different gross profit rates to the segments because of factors such as different levels of risk or differences in the relationship of the supply and demand for the services provided in different segments.
4. The contractor has a significant history of providing similar services to other customers under separate contracts for each significant segment to which a profit margin higher than the overall profit margin on the project is ascribed.
5. The significant history with customers who have contracted for services separately is one that is relatively stable in terms of pric-

ing policy rather than one unduly weighted by erratic pricing decisions (responding, for example, to extraordinary economic circumstances or to unique customer-contractor relationships).

6. The excess of the sum of the prices of the separate elements over the price of the total project is clearly attributable to cost savings incident to combined performance of the contract obligations (for example, cost savings in supervision, overhead, or equipment mobilization). Unless this condition is met, segmenting a contract with a price substantially less than the sum of the prices of the separate phases or elements is inappropriate even if the other conditions are met. Acceptable price variations are allocated to the separate phases or elements in proportion to the prices ascribed to each. In all other situations, a substantial difference in price (whether more or less) between the separate elements and the price of the total project is evidence that the contractor has accepted different profit margins. Accordingly, segmenting is not appropriate, and the contracts are the profit centers.

7. The similarity of services and prices in the contract segments and services and the prices of such services to other customers contracted separately are documented and verifiable.

Note that the criteria for combining and segmenting are to be applied consistently to contracts with similar characteristics and in similar circumstances.

Joint Ventures and Shared Contracts

Especially large or risky contracts are sometimes shared by more than one contractor. When the owner of the contract requests competitive bids, many contractors will form syndicates or joint ventures in order to bid on and successfully obtain a contract that each contractor individually could not perform.

When this occurs, a separate set of accounting records is maintained for the joint venture. If the percentages of interest for each of the participants are identical in more than one contract, the joint venture might keep its records in the same manner as it would if it was simply another construction company. Usually the joint venture is for a single contract and ends upon completion of that contract.

A joint venture is a type of partnership, organized for a limited purpose. An agreement of the parties and the terms of the contract successfully bid upon will determine the nature of the accounting records. Income statements are usually cumulative statements showing totals from date of contract inception until reporting date. Each participant records its share of the amount from the venture's income statement less its previously recorded portion of the venture's income as a single line item similar to the equity method for investments. Similarly, balance sheets of each participant present a single line asset balance, "investment in and advances to joint ventures." In most cases, footnote disclosure is similar to the equity method and presents condensed financial statements of material joint ventures.

Accounting for Change Orders

Change orders are modifications of specifications or provisions of an original contract. Contract revenue and costs are adjusted to reflect change orders that are approved by the contractor and customer. Accounting for a change order depends on the scope and price of the change.

If the scope and price have both been agreed to by the customer and contractor, contract revenue and cost are both adjusted to reflect the change order.

Accounting for unpriced change orders depends on their characteristics and the circumstances in which they occur. Under the completed-contract method, costs attributable to unpriced change orders are deferred as contract costs if it is probable that total contract costs, including costs attributable to the change orders, will be recovered from contract revenues. Recovery is deemed probable if the future event or events are likely to occur.

The following guidelines apply when accounting for unpriced change orders under the percentage-of-completion method:

1. If it is not probable that the costs will be recovered through a change in the contract price, costs attributable to unpriced change orders are treated as costs of contract performance in the period in which the costs are incurred.
2. If it is probable that the costs will be recovered through a change in the contract price, the costs are deferred (excluded from the costs of contract performance) until the parties have agreed on the change in contract price, or, alternatively, treated as costs of contract performance in the period in which they are incurred with a corresponding increase to contract revenue in the amount of the costs incurred.
3. If it is probable that the contract price will be adjusted by an amount that exceeds the costs attributable to the change order and both of the following apply:
    a. If the amount of the excess can be reliably estimated, and
    b. Realization of the full contract price adjustment is probable beyond a reasonable doubt,

then the original contract price is adjusted for the full amount of the adjustment as the costs are recognized.

However, since the substantiation of the amount of future revenue is difficult, satisfaction of the condition of "realization beyond a reasonable doubt" should be considered satisfied only in circumstances in which an entity's historical experience provides such assurance or in which an entity has received a bona fide pricing offer from a customer and records only the amount of the offer as revenue.

Accounting for Contract Options

An addition or option to an existing contract is treated as a separate contract if any of the following circumstances exist:

1. The product or service to be provided differs significantly from the product or service provided under the original contract.
2. The price of the new product or service is negotiated without regard to the original contract and involves different economic judgments.
3. The products or services to be provided under the exercised option or amendment are similar to those under the original contract, but the contract price and anticipated contract cost relationship are significantly different.

If the addition or option does not meet the preceding circumstances, the contracts are combined unless the addition or option does not meet the criteria for combining, in which case it is treated as a change order.

Accounting for Claims

Claims represent amounts in excess of the agreed-upon contract price that a contractor seeks to collect from customers for unanticipated additional costs. The recognition of additional contract revenue relating to claims is appropriate if it is probable that the claim will result in additional revenue and if the amount can be reliably estimated. All of the following conditions must exist in order for the probable and estimable requirements to be satisfied:

1. The contract or other evidence provides a legal basis for the claim; or a legal opinion has been obtained, stating that under the circumstances there is a reasonable basis to support the claim.
2. Additional costs are caused by circumstances that were unforeseen at the contract date and are not the result of deficiencies in the contractor's performance.

3. Costs associated with the claim are identifiable or otherwise deter-minable and are reasonable in view of the work performed.
4. The evidence supporting the claim is objective and verifiable, not based on management's "feel" for the situation or on unsupported representations.

When the above requirements are met, revenue from a claim is re-corded only to the extent that contract costs relating to the claim have been incurred.

Accounting Changes

A change in method of accounting for long-term construction contracts is a special change in principle requiring retroactive treatment and re-statement of previous financial statements.

Revisions in revenue, cost, and profit estimates or in measurements of the extent of progress toward completion are changes in accounting esti-mates. These changes are accounted for prospectively in order for the fi-nancial statements to fully reflect the effects of the latest available esti-mates.

Long-Term Construction Contract Disclosures

A company should disclose the methods it uses to determine revenue, so in this case it should itemize its use of either the percentage-of-completion or the completed-contract method. Also, the methods used to measure the extent of progress toward completion of a project should be disclosed. Further, the specific criteria used to determine when a contract is substantially completed should be disclosed. An example follows:

> The company recognizes all revenue in its construction division using the percentage-of-completion method, under which it ascertains the completion percentage by dividing costs incurred to date by total estimated project costs. It revises estimated project costs regularly, which can alter the reported level of project profitability. If project losses are calculated under this method, they are recognized in the current reporting period. Claims against customers are recorded in the period when payment is received. If billings exceed rec-ognized revenue, the difference is recorded as a current liability, while any recognized revenues exceeding billings are recorded as a current asset.

In addition, a company should disclose any material revenue increases caused by claims in excess of the original contract amounts, which may also require the disclosure of a contingent asset, if the amount of the claims exceeds the recorded contract costs. An example follows:

> The company recognizes claims against customers when cash receipt is probable, the claim is legally justified, and the amount of the claim can be proven. If any of these factors cannot be reasonably proven, then claims are

only recognized upon the receipt of cash. Since claims involve the use of estimates, it is reasonable to record some changes to the initially reported revenue figure upon the eventual receipt of cash, or sooner if there is a firm basis for this information.

Another disclosure is to note the effect of significant revisions in estimates on recorded revenue levels.

If there is a change in the method of contract revenue recognition, the reason for doing so should be revealed, as well as the net effect of the change. An example follows:

> The company has switched to the percentage-of-completion method from the completed-contract method for recording the results of its construction projects. Management authorized the change due to the increasingly long-term nature of its contracts, which have increased from single-month to multimonth durations. The net impact of this change was an increase in profits of $218,000 in 2010. The change was carried back to 2006, resulting in a profit increase of $12,000 in that period.

Long-Term Construction Contract Policies and Procedures

An accounting policy should state that all construction contract revenue be calculated using just one of the two primary revenue recognition methods (e.g., the percentage-of-completion or completed-contract methods). This policy allows a company to calculate all construction revenues using a consistent methodology, so there is no question of using one method over another to gain a short-term advantage in reporting the amount of revenue.

Another accounting policy should specify that accounts used in overhead cost pools be reviewed annually and altered only with written management approval. This policy keeps the accounting staff from arbitrarily altering the contents of overhead cost pools. Overhead pool alterations are a classic approach for shifting expenses out of the current period and into construction-in-progress asset accounts.

The following procedure can be used to determine the amount of revenue to be recognized on a construction project:

1. Access the approved project bid file and determine the estimated gross profit percentage for the project.
2. Discuss the estimated gross margin with the project manager to verify that the percentage is still valid. If not, use the project manager's revised estimate.
3. Access the general ledger and note the total amount of expenses accumulated to date in the project's Construction-in-Progress account.

4. Divide the total project expenses by one minus the estimated gross profit percentage to arrive at total expenses plus the estimated gross profit.
5. Access the project billing records and determine the total amount of billings made to the customer thus far.
6. Subtract the total expenses and estimated gross profit from the billings figure. If the amount of expenses and gross profits is larger than the billed amount, debit the Unbilled Contract Receivables account and credit the Contract Revenues Earned account for the difference. If the amount of expenses and gross profits is less than the billed amount, debit the Contract Revenues Earned account and credit the Billings Exceeding Project Costs and Margin account for the difference.

Long-Term Construction Contract Controls

There are a large number of areas in which the calculation of construction-related revenue can be altered to result in significant changes to the reported level of revenue. The following bullet points contain a number of controls designed to prevent or detect such revenue alterations:

- **Compare the declared percentage of completion to estimated work required to complete projects.** A very common way to record excessive revenue on a construction project is to falsely state that the percentage of completion is greater than the actual figure, thereby allowing the company to record a greater proportion of revenues in the current period. Though difficult to verify with any precision, a reasonable control is to match the declared percentage of completion to a percentage of the actual hours worked, divided by the total estimated number of hours worked. The two percentages should match.
- **Ensure that project expenses are charged to the correct account.** A common problem with revenue recognition under the percentage-of-completion method is that extra expenses may be erroneously or falsely loaded into a project's general ledger account, which can then be used as the justification for the recognition of additional revenue related to that project. Auditing expenses in active project accounts can spot these problems.
- **Promptly close project accounts once projects are completed.** It is not a difficult matter to incorrectly store project-related expenses in the wrong accounts, and may be done fraudulently in order to avoid recognizing losses related to excessive amounts of expenses being incurred on specific projects. This problem can be resolved by

promptly closing general ledger project accounts once the related projects are complete. Closing project accounts can be included in the month-end closing procedure, thereby ensuring that this problem will be addressed on a regular basis.

- **Control access to general ledger accounts.** Employees are less likely to shift expenses between general ledger construction accounts if they are unable to access the accounts, or if they have no way of reopening closed accounts. This can be achieved by tightly restricting account access, and especially access to the closed or open status flag for each account.

- **Compare the dates on supplier invoices in the Construction-in-Progress account to the project start date.** Since precontract costs must be charged to expense, there is a temptation to hold these supplier invoices until after the project contract has been signed, so they can be stored in the Construction-in-Progress account rather than as an asset. To detect this problem, examine a selection of invoiced expenses in the account to see if any are dated prior to the project's contract date.

- **Review journal entries shifting expenses into Construction-in-Progress accounts.** Since precontract costs must be charged to expense, there is a temptation to increase short-term profits by shifting these expenses into the Construction-in-Progress account with a journal entry. To spot this problem, review all journal entries adding expenses to the Construction-in-Progress account.

- **Consistently aggregate expenses into overhead accounts and charge them to individual projects.** One could charge different overhead expenses to various projects or apply the same pool of overhead costs inconsistently to the accounts, thereby effectively shifting expenses to those projects that would result in the greatest revenue increase under the percentage-of-completion revenue recognition method. To avoid this problem, periodically verify that the same expenses are being consistently charged to overhead cost pools over time and that the same allocation method is used to shift these expenses from the overhead cost pools to project accounts.

- **Exclude the cost of unused materials from cost-to-cost percentage-of-completion calculations.** More materials than are initially needed are typically purchased at the beginning of a project. This increases the amount of recognizable revenue early in a project when the cost-to-cost percentage-of-completion method is used. To avoid this problem, remove all unused materials from the calculation.

- **Compare the percentage of revenues recognized with expenses recognized.** When revenues associated with a project are recognized, one must also make a second entry to shift costs from the Construction-in-Progress account to the cost of goods sold. If this second entry is missed for any reason, profits will be unusually high. To spot this problem, compare the amount of recognized revenue to recognized expenses for each project and verify that it matches the most recent gross profit estimate for the project. If the percentage is higher, some expenses have probably not been recognized.

- **Review prospective project issues with the construction manager.** A common fraud involving project accounting is to shift the timing and amount of recognized losses on projects. These losses can be delayed in order to make the current period's results look better, or made excessively large or small in order to meet reporting targets. Though it is quite difficult to ascertain if the size of a loss is correct, it is possible to guess *when* a loss should be recognized. By having regular discussions with a project's construction manager regarding ongoing and upcoming project-related issues, it is possible to see when significant unbudgeted costs are to be incurred, thereby giving some insight into the need for loss recognition.

- **Watch for expense loading on cost-plus contracts.** When a company is guaranteed by the customer to pay for all expenses incurred, there exists a temptation to load extra expenses into an account. These expense additions can be spotted by looking for charges from suppliers whose costs are not normally charged to a specific type of contract, as well as by looking for expense types that increase significantly over expenses incurred in previous periods, and by investigating any journal entries that increase expense levels.

8 REVENUE RECOGNITION FOR MOTION PICTURES

OVERVIEW

Due to the uncertainties involved in estimating the revenues that will be earned and costs that will be incurred over a film's life, a particular estimation methodology is used to achieve proper matching of costs and revenues and accurately reflect the results of the film's financial performance.

The term *film* is generic and includes intellectual property produced on traditional celluloid film as well as videotape, digital, or other video-recording formats. The content or format of films includes (1) feature films, (2) television series, (3) television specials, and (4) similar products (including animated films and television programming).

There are many varieties of contractual sales or licensing arrangements governing the rights or group of rights to a single or multiple films. The film's producer (referred to as "the entity") may license it to distributors, theaters, exhibitors, or other licensees (referred to as "customers") on an exclusive or nonexclusive basis in a particular market or territory. The terms of the license may be for a fixed (or flat) fee or the fee may be variable based on a percentage of the customer's revenue. If the arrangement is variable, it may include a nonrefundable minimum guarantee payable either in advance or over the licensing period.

DEFINITIONS OF TERMS

Cross-collateralized. A contractual arrangement granting distribution rights to multiple films, territories, and/or markets to a licensee. In this type of arrangement, the exploitation results of the entire package are aggregated by the licensee in determining amounts payable to the licensor.

Distributor. The owner or holder of the rights to distribute films. Excluded from this definition are entities that function solely as broadcasters, retailers (such as video stores), or movie theaters.

Exploitation costs. All direct costs incurred in connection with the film's distribution. Examples include marketing, advertising, publicity, promotion, and other distribution expenses.

Film costs. Film costs include all direct negative costs incurred in the physical production of a film, including allocations of production overhead and capitalized interest. Examples of direct negative costs include costs of story and scenario; compensation of cast members, extras, directors, producers, and miscellaneous staff; costs of set construction and operations, wardrobe and accessories; costs of sound synchronization; rental facilities on location; and postproduction costs such as music, special effects, and editing.

Film prints. The materials containing the completed audio and video elements of a film, which are distributed to a theater to exhibit the film to its customers.

Firm commitment. An agreement with a third party that is binding on both parties. The agreement specifies all significant terms, including items to be exchanged, consideration, and timing of the transaction. The agreement includes a disincentive for nonperformance that is sufficiently large to ensure the expected performance. With respect to an episodic television series, a firm commitment for future production includes only episodes to be delivered within one year from the date of the estimate of ultimate revenue.

Market. A distribution channel located within a certain geographic territory for a certain type of media, exhibition, or related product. Examples include theatrical exhibition, home video (such as DVD or Blu-Ray), pay television, free television, and the licensing of film-related merchandise.

Nonrefundable minimum guarantee. Amount to be paid by a customer in a variable fee arrangement that guarantees an entity a minimum fee on that arrangement. This amount applies to payments paid at inception, as well as to legally binding commitments to pay amounts over the license period.

Overall deal. An arrangement whereby an entity compensates a creative individual (e.g., producer, actor, or director) for the exclusive or preferential use of that party's creative services.

Participation costs. Frequently, persons involved in the production of a film are compensated, in part or in full, with an interest (referred to as "participation") in the financial results of the film. Determination of the amount of compensation payable to the participant is usually based on formulas (participations) and by contingent amounts due under provisions of collective bargaining agreements (residuals). The recipients of this compensation are referred to as participants and the costs are referred to as participation costs. Participations may be paid to creative talent (e.g., actors or writers) or to entities from whom distribution rights are licensed.

Producer. An individual or enterprise that is responsible for all aspects of a film. Although the producer's role may vary, his or her responsibilities include administration of such aspects of the project as initial concept, script, budgeting, shooting, postproduction, and release.

Revenue. Amounts earned by an entity from its direct distribution, exploitation, or licensing of a film, before deduction for any of the entity's direct costs of distribution. In markets and territories where the entity's fully or jointly owned films are distributed by third-party distributors, revenue is the net amount payable to the entity by the distributor. Revenue is reduced by appropriate allowances, estimated returns, price concessions, or similar adjustments, as applicable.

Sale. The transfer of control of the master copy of a film and all of the associated rights that accompany it.

Set for production. A film qualifies as being set for production when all of the following conditions have been met: (1) management with relevant authority authorizes (implicitly or explicitly) and commits to funding the film's production; (2) active preproduction has begun; and (3) the start of principal photography is expected to begin within six months.

Territory. A geographic area in which a film is exploited, usually a country. In some cases, however, a territory may be contractually defined as countries with a common language.

REVENUE RECOGNITION

An entity recognizes revenue from a sale or licensing arrangement only when all of the following conditions are met:

1. Persuasive evidence exists of a sale or licensing arrangement with a customer.
2. The film is complete and, in accordance with the terms of the arrangement, has been delivered or is available for immediate and unconditional delivery.
3. The license period for the arrangement has started and the customer can begin exploitation, exhibition, or sale.
4. The arrangement fee is fixed or determinable.
5. Collection of the arrangement fee is reasonably assured.

If any of the above conditions has not been met, the entity defers recognizing revenue until all of the conditions are met. If the entity recognizes a receivable on its balance sheet for advances under an arrangement for which all of the above conditions have not been met, a liability for deferred revenue of the same amount is to be recognized until such time as all of the conditions have been met. The preceding list of conditions is discussed in the following bullet points:

1. **Persuasive evidence of an arrangement.** This condition is met solely by documentary evidence that sets forth, at a minimum, the following terms: (1) the license period, (2) the film or films covered by the agreement, (3) a description of the rights transferred, and (4) the consideration to be exchanged. If the agreement is ambiguous regarding the parties' rights and obligations, or if there is significant doubt as to the ability of either party to perform under the agreement, revenue is not recognized. Acceptable documentary evidence must be verifiable (e.g., a contract, a purchase order, or an online authorization).

2. **Delivery.** The delivery condition may be satisfied by an arrangement providing the customer with immediate and unconditional access to a film print held by the entity. The customer may also receive a lab access letter that authorizes it to order a film laboratory to make the film immediately and unconditionally available for its use. Under these conditions, the delivery condition is satisfied if the film is complete and available for immediate delivery.

   Some licensing arrangements require the entity to make significant changes to the film after it becomes initially available. Significant changes are changes that are additive to the film and that result from the entity creating additional content after the film becomes initially available. The changes can consist of the reshooting of selected scenes or adding additional special effects. When such changes are required to be made to the film, the arrangement does not meet the delivery condition. The costs incurred for these significant changes are added to film costs and subsequently recorded as expense when the related revenue is recognized.

   Changes that are not considered to be significant changes include insertion or addition of preexisting film footage, addition of dubbing or subtitles to existing footage, removal of offensive language, reformatting to fit a broadcaster's screen dimensions, or adjustments to allow for the insertion of television commercials. Such insignificant changes do not alter the film's qualification to meet the delivery condition. The expected costs of these insignificant changes are accrued and charged directly to expense by the entity at the time that revenue recognition commences even if they have not yet been incurred.

3. **Commencement of exploitation.** Some arrangements impose on the customer a release date or "street date" before which the film may not be exhibited or sold. Such a date defines the commencement date of the exploitation rights. The entity does not begin to recognize revenue on the arrangement until this restriction has expired.

4. **Fixed or determinable arrangement fee.** When there is a flat fee that covers a single film, the amount of the fee is considered fixed and determinable and the entity recognizes the entire license fee as revenue when all of the conditions set forth above have been satisfied.

   If the flat fee applies to multiple films, some of which have not been produced or completed, the entity allocates the fee to each individual film by market or territory based on relative fair values of the rights to exploit each film under the licensing arrangement. The entity bases the allocations to a film or films not yet produced or completed on the amounts that would be refundable if the entity did not ultimately complete and deliver the films to the customer. The entity allocates the remaining flat fee to completed films based on the relative fair values of the exploitation rights to those films under the arrangement. These allocations may not be adjusted subsequently even if better information becomes available. After making the allocations described above, the entity recognizes revenue for each film when all of the above conditions are met with respect to that film by market and territory. If the entity is not able to determine relative fair values for the exploitation rights, then the fee is not fixed or determinable and the entity may not recognize revenue until such a determination can be made and it meets all five of the conditions.

   An entity's arrangement fees may be variable based on a percentage of the customer's revenue from exploitation of the film. When all five conditions have been met, the entity commences revenue recognition as the customer exploits or exhibits the film.

   Certain variable fee arrangements include a nonrefundable minimum guarantee whereby the customer guarantees to pay the entity a nonrefundable minimum amount that is applied against the variable fees on a film or group of films that are not cross-collateralized. In applying the revenue recognition conditions, the amount of the nonrefundable minimum guarantee is considered to be fixed and determinable and is recognized as revenue when all of the other conditions have been met. If the nonrefundable minimum guarantee is applied against variable fees from a group of films on a cross-collateralized basis, the amount of the minimum guarantee attributable to each individual film cannot be objectively determined. In this situation, the entity recognizes revenue as described in the preceding paragraph (i.e., when all five of the conditions have been met as the customer exhibits or exploits each film). Under this scenario, if there is a remaining portion of the nonrefundable minimum guarantee that is unearned at the end of the license period, the entity recognizes the remaining guarantee as revenue by allocating it to the individual films based on their relative performance under the arrangement.

5. **Returns and price concessions** can affect whether the arrangement fee meets the condition of being fixed and determinable. The factors to consider include the provisions of the arrangement between the entity and its customer and the entity's policies and past actions related to granting concessions or accepting product returns. If the arrangement includes a right-of-return provision or if its past practices allow for such rights, the entity must be able to reasonably estimate the amount of future returns.

MODIFICATIONS OF ARRANGEMENTS

If, during the term of a licensing arrangement, the entity and its customer agree to extend an existing arrangement for which all of the revenue recognition conditions have been met, the accounting follows the same rules cited above for flat-fee arrangements, variable fee arrangements, and variable fee arrangements with minimum guarantees.

For modifications that are not extensions of an existing arrangement, the modification is accounted for as a new arrangement and a termination of the former arrangement. At the time the former arrangement is terminated, the entity accrues and expenses all costs associated with the arrangement or reverses previously reported revenue to reflect refunds and concessions that result from the new arrangement. In addition, the entity adjusts accumulated film cost amortization and accrued participation costs attributable to the excess revenue.

Example

Eva Enterprises produced a film that did not meet revenue expectations. The film was originally projected to gross $9,500,000 and to date has only earned $2,300,000.

The original arrangement called for a fixed fee of $150,000. Eva had previously met all five criteria for recognizing the $150,000 fixed fee as revenue. To placate its customers, Eva negotiates a new arrangement that reduces the original fixed fee from $150,000 to $80,000 and substitutes a variable component based on 1% of the customers' revenues from exploiting the film. The effects of the new arrangement on Eva's revenue are computed as follows:

Revenue recognizable under new arrangement	
Fixed fee	$ 80,000
Variable fee earned to date (1% of $2,300,000)	23,000
	103,000
Original fixed fee recognized as revenue	150,000
Reduction in revenue due to new arrangement	$(47,000)

In addition to the adjustment above, Eva also must adjust its previously recorded accumulated amortization of film costs and accrued participation costs attributable to the excess revenue previously recorded.

PRODUCT LICENSING

Any revenue from licensing arrangements to market film-related products is deferred until the release date of the film.

PRESENT VALUE

Revenue that an entity recognizes in connection with licensing arrangements is recorded at the present value of the license fee as of the date that the entity first recognizes the revenue.

Example

Eva Enterprises produces a film for which it meets all revenue recognition criteria as of January 1, 2010, with a payment schedule of $30,000 to be paid on January 1, 2010, $40,000 to be paid on January 1, 2011, and $50,000 to be paid on January 1, 2012. The appropriate interest rate for the calculation of interest is 8% per year. Eva recognizes revenue and interest income in accordance with the following schedule:

Year	Payment	Present Value Multiple	Present Value	Revenue Recognition	Interest Income
2010	$ 30,000	1.00000	$ 30,000	$109,904	$ 6,392[a]
2011	$ 40,000	0.92593	$ 37,037	—	$ 3,704[b]
2012	$ 50,000	0.85734	$ 42,867	—	—
	$120,000		$109,904	$109,904	$10,096

[a] *8% interest on $79,904 present value of second ($40,000) and third ($50,000) payments*

[b] *8% interest on $46,297 present value of final $50,000 payment*

MOTION PICTURE REVENUE DISCLOSURES

An entity should disclose its methods of accounting for revenue. Sample disclosures are as follows:

- Revenue from the sale of home video units is recognized at the later of when product is made available for retail sale or when video sales to customers are reported by third parties, such as fulfillment service providers or distributors. Management calculates an estimate of future returns of product by analyzing a combination of historical returns, current economic trends, projections of consumer demand for the company's product, and point-of-sale data available from certain retailers. Based on this information, a percentage of each sale is reserved, provided that the customer has the right of return. Actual returns are charged against the reserve.

- Long-term noninterest-bearing receivables arising from television licensing agreements are discounted to present value, net of an allowance for doubtful accounts.

- The company recognizes revenues from its films net of reserves for returns, rebates, and other incentives after it has retained a distribution fee of ___ % and recovered all of its distribution and marketing costs on a title-by-title basis.

9 REVENUE RECOGNITION FOR NOT-FOR-PROFITS

DEFINITIONS OF TERMS

Contribution. An unconditional transfer of assets to an entity or settlement of its liabilities in a voluntary nonreciprocal transfer.

Collections. Works of art or similar assets that are held for public use, protected, and subject to an entity's policy to use any proceeds from their sale to acquire new assets for the collection.

Donor-imposed condition. A specification of a future and uncertain event whose occurrence or failure to occur gives the donor the right of return of the contributed assets.

Donor-imposed restriction. A specification of the use to which a donated asset may be put.

Nonreciprocal transfer. When an entity incurs a liability or transfers away an asset while not receiving anything in exchange.

Permanent restriction. A donor-imposed restriction stipulating that resources be maintained permanently, though allowing alternative use of the income derived from the resources.

Promise to give. An agreement to give an asset to another entity.

NOT-FOR-PROFIT REVENUE RECOGNITION

Revenues are reported in the statement of activities as increases in unrestricted net assets unless the use of the resources received is subject to a donor-imposed restriction. Thus, contribution revenues increase unrestricted net assets, temporarily restricted net assets, or permanently restricted net assets, depending on the existence and nature of donors' restrictions. Revenues from most exchange transactions (such as sales of goods or services) are classified as unrestricted.

Revenues from exchange transactions increase restricted net asset classes only if a preexisting donor-imposed restriction limits the use of the resources received. For example, if a donor contributes a car to the local library and requires that the proceeds from the sale of the car be used to purchase children's books, the proceeds from the sale of the car (an exchange transaction) increase temporarily restricted net assets. Investment income and gains (which are also exchange transactions) increase unrestricted net assets unless a donor required that the gift be invested and the investment return used for a restricted purpose. For example, assume a donor contributes securities worth $85,000 to a zoo, requires that all dividends and gains be retained and reinvested until the accumulated value is $100,000, and states that the $100,000 must be maintained as a permanent endowment fund, the income of which is to be used for the purchase of animals. In the early years of the endowment, before the accumulated value reaches $100,000, investment income and gains increase permanently restricted net assets. Investment income and gains earned after the accumulated value of the fund reaches $100,000 increase temporarily restricted net assets with the restriction expiring upon use of those funds to purchase animals.

Contributions should be recognized as revenue at the time of the gift and measured at the fair value of the contributed assets regardless of the form of the assets contributed. Donor-imposed restrictions do not change the timing of recognition of a contribution. Donor-imposed restrictions, or the absence of them, affect only a contribution's classification as an increase in permanently restricted net assets, temporarily restricted net assets, or unrestricted net assets. Donor-imposed conditions, however, affect the timing of recognition. Because a contribution is an unconditional transfer, a transfer of assets subject to donor-imposed conditions is not a contribution yet, although it may become one at a future date. Conditional transfers are not recognized as contribution revenues until the conditions are substantially met. Thus, the distinction between donor-imposed restrictions and donor-imposed conditions is very important to the timing of recognition. If a donor's stipulations do not clearly state whether a gift depends on meeting a stated stipulation and the ambiguity cannot be resolved by communicating with the donor or by examining the circumstances surrounding the gift, a transfer is presumed to be conditional.

Unconditional promises to give cash or other assets are recognized in financial statements when the promise is made and received, provided that there is sufficient evidence in the form of verifiable documentation (written, audio, or video). If payments of the promises are due in future periods, the promise has an implied time restriction that expires on the date the payment is due. Thus, unless circumstances surrounding the receipt of the promise indicate that the donor intended the gift to support the current period's activities, unconditional promises increase temporarily restricted net assets. The present value of estimated future cash flows is used to measure unconditional promises to give, although short-term promises (due in less than one year) may be reported at net realizable value. Conditional promises are not recognized as revenue until the conditions are substantially met.

In a manner similar to recognizing promises to give, a beneficiary recognizes contributions held on its behalf by an agent, trustee, or intermediary. For example, if the assets held by the agent were transferred subject to a condition that is not yet met, the beneficiary does not recognize its potential rights to the assets held by the agent. If a beneficiary has an unconditional right to receive cash flows from a charitable trust or other pool of assets, the beneficiary recognizes its rights when the beneficial interest is created and measures the rights using the present value of the estimated expected cash flows. However, if the beneficiary and the agent, trustee, or intermediary are financially interrelated organizations, the beneficiary reports its rights to the assets held using a method similar to the equity method of accounting for investments.

The value of volunteer services received by the organization is recognized in certain circumstances. Contributed services that create or improve a nonfinancial asset (such as building a shed or replacing a roof) are recognized as revenue as contributions either by valuing the hours of service received or by measuring the change in the fair value of the nonfinancial asset created or improved. Other contributed services are recognized only if they meet all three of the following criteria: (1) they require specialized skills, (2) they are provided by persons possessing those skills, and (3) they would typically need to be purchased if not provided by donation. If volunteer services neither meet those three criteria nor create or improve nonfinancial assets, they cannot be recognized in the organization's financial statements.

An organization that maintains works of art, historical treasures, and similar assets in collections does not recognize gifts of items that are added to its collections unless it also capitalizes its collections. However, gifts that are not added to collections or items given to organizations that do not maintain collections are recognized as revenues and measured at the fair value of the assets received.

NOT-FOR-PROFIT REVENUE DISCLOSURES

Unconditional promises to give assets to a not-for-profit must be disclosed in the notes to the financial statements. This disclosure shall include the amounts of promises receivable in less than one year, in one to five years, and in more than five years. Disclosure shall also be made of the amount of the allowance for uncollectible promises receivable.

Conditional promises to give assets to a not-for-profit must be disclosed in the notes to the financial statements. This disclosure shall include the total of the amounts promised and a description and amount for each group of promises having similar characteristics (such as promises conditioned on the receipt of matching funds).

Organizations are required to describe the programs or activities for which contributed services are used and the nature and extent of services received for the period (regardless of whether those services are recognized), and disclose the amount recognized as revenues.

NOT-FOR-PROFIT REVENUE POLICIES AND PROCEDURES

Contributions should be measured at their fair value. This can be a highly subjective measurement that varies considerably by contribution, so a policy should be used to standardize the measurement system. This policy should require formal appraisal of the value of contributions exceeding an estimated monetary threshold, while stipulating that contributions received that are below this threshold are assigned a fair value using a rigidly defined set of evaluation criteria.

A similar policy should be used for the valuation of volunteer services provided, since the conversion of these services into reported revenue can be subject to a great deal of interpretation. The policy should define the rules under which these services are to be recognized as revenue and how the hours of service are to be valued.

NOT-FOR-PROFIT REVENUE CONTROLS

The key issue with not-for-profit revenue recognition is the proper interpretation of donor-imposed conditions, since their related contributions cannot be recognized as revenue until the conditions are met. Thus, an important control is a periodic review of the documents containing donor conditions to ensure that the conditions have been met and that recognition occurred in the proper reporting period.

Additional controls should be implemented to review the adequacy of an organization's application of policies to measure contributions, both of assets and volunteer services, as described in the preceding section.

10 REVENUE RECOGNITION ON REAL ESTATE SALES

OVERVIEW

The substance of a sale of any asset is that the transaction unconditionally transfers the risks and rewards of ownership to the buyer. However, the economic substance of many real estate sales is that the risks and rewards of ownership have not been clearly transferred. The turbulent and cyclical environments in the real estate and debt markets have led to the evolution of many complex methods of financing real estate transactions. For example, in some transactions the seller, rather than an independent third party, finances the buyer, while in others, the seller may be required to guarantee a minimum return to the buyer or continue to operate the property for a specified period of time. In many of these complex transactions, the seller still has some association with the property even after the property has been sold. The question that must be answered in these transactions is: At what point does the seller become disassociated enough from the property that profit may be recognized on the transaction?

DEFINITIONS OF TERMS

Continuing investment. Payments that the buyer is contractually required to pay on its total debt for the purchase price of the property.

Cost recovery method. A method that defers the recognition of gross profit on a real estate sale until the seller recovers the cost of the property sold.

Deposit method. A method that records payments by the buyer as deposits rather than a sale. The seller continues to report the asset and related debt on the balance sheet until the contract is canceled or until the sale has been achieved.

First mortgage (primary debt). The senior debt the seller has on the property at the time the buyer purchases the property. A first mortgage lender (mortgagee) has foreclosure rights superior to those of second (or junior) mortgage lenders (i.e., proceeds from sale of the foreclosed property are used first to repay the first mortgage lender in full with only the remainder available to satisfy the junior lenders' balances).

Full accrual method. A method that recognizes all profit from a real estate sale at the time of sale.

Initial investment. The sales value received by the seller at the time of sale. It includes a cash down payment, buyer's notes supported by an irrevocable letter of credit, and payments by the buyer to third parties to reduce or eliminate the seller's indebtedness on the property.

Installment method. A method that recognizes revenue on the basis of payments made by the buyer on debt owed to the seller and payments by the buyer to the holder of primary debt. Each payment is apportioned between profit and cost recovery.

Lien. A claim or charge a creditor has on property that serves as security for payment of debt by the debtor.

Minimum initial investment. The minimum amount that an initial investment must equal or exceed so that the criterion for using the full accrual method is met.

Partial sale. A sale in which the seller retains an equity interest in the property or has an equity interest in the buyer.

Property improvements. An addition made to real estate, usually consisting of buildings but that may also include any permanent structure such as streets, sidewalks, sewers, utilities, and so on.

Reduced profit method. A method that recognizes profit at the point of sale, but only a reduced amount. The remaining profit is deferred to future periods.

Release provision. An agreement that provides for the release of property to the buyer. This agreement releases the property to the buyer free of any previous liens.

Sales value. The sales price of the property increased or decreased for other consideration in the sales transaction that are, in substance, additional sales proceeds to the seller.

Subordination. The process by which a party's rights are ranked below the rights of others.

REAL ESTATE SALES OTHER THAN RETAIL LAND SALES

Profit Recognition Methods

Profit from real estate sales is recognized in full, provided the following:

1. The profit is determinable (i.e., the collectibility of the sales price is reasonably assured or the amount that will not be collectible can be estimated).

2. The earnings process is virtually complete, that is, the seller is not obliged to perform significant activities after the sale to earn the profit.

When both of these conditions are satisfied, the method used to recognize profits on real estate sales is referred to as the full accrual method. If both of these conditions are not satisfied, recognition of all or part of the profit is postponed.

For real estate sales, the collectibility of the sales price is reasonably assured when the buyer has demonstrated a commitment to pay. This commitment is supported by a substantial initial investment, along with continuing investments that give the buyer a sufficient stake in the property such that the risk of loss through default motivates the buyer to honor its obligations to the seller. Collectibility of the sales price is also assessed by examining the conditions surrounding the sale (e.g., credit history of the buyer; age, condition, and location of the property; and history of cash flows generated by the property).

The full accrual method is appropriate and profit is recognized in full at the point of sale for real estate transactions when all of the following criteria are met:

1. A sale is consummated.
2. The buyer's initial and continuing investments are adequate to demonstrate a commitment to pay for the property.
3. The seller's receivable is not subject to future subordination.
4. The seller has transferred to the buyer the usual risks and rewards of ownership in a transaction that is in substance a sale, and the seller does not have a substantial continuing involvement in the property.

On sales in which an independent third party provides all of the financing for the buyer, the seller is most concerned that criterion 1 is met. For such sales, the sale is usually consummated on the closing date. When the seller finances the buyer, the seller must analyze the economic substance of the agreement to ascertain that criteria 2, 3, and 4 are also met (i.e., whether the transaction clearly transfers the risks and rewards of ownership to the buyer).

The seller of real estate should follow these guidelines when considering the various forms of financing that may be applicable to the transaction:

1. Obtaining sufficient initial and continuing investment from the buyer before full accrual profit recognition is allowed must be ap-

plied unless the seller receives the full sales value of the property including

    a. Cash without any seller contingent liability on any debt on the property incurred or assumed by the buyer,

    b. The buyer's assumption of the seller's existing nonrecourse debt on the property,

    c. The buyer's assumption of all recourse debt on the property with the complete release of the seller from those obligations, or

    d. Any combination of such cash and debt assumption.

2. In computing the buyer's initial investment, debt incurred by the buyer that is secured by the property is not considered part of the buyer's initial investment. This is true whether the debt was incurred directly from the seller or other parties or indirectly through assumption. Payments to the seller from the proceeds of such indebtedness are not included as part of the buyer's initial investment.

3. If the transaction does not qualify for full accrual accounting and, consequently, is being accounted for using installment, cost recovery or reduced profit methods, payments made on debt described in item 2. are not considered to be buyer's cash payments. However, if the profit deferred under the applicable method exceeds the outstanding amount of seller financing and the outstanding amount of buyer's debt secured by the property for which the seller is contingently liable, the seller recognizes the excess in income.

Consummation of a Sale

A sale is considered consummated when the following conditions are met:

1. The parties are bound by the terms of a contract.
2. All consideration has been exchanged.
3. Any permanent financing for which the seller is responsible has been arranged.
4. All conditions precedent to closing have been performed.

When a seller is constructing office buildings, condominiums, shopping centers, or similar structures, item 4. may be applied to individual units rather than the entire project. These four conditions are usually met on or after closing, not at the point the agreement to sell is signed or at a preclosing meeting. Closing refers to the final steps of the transaction (i.e., when consideration is paid, the mortgage is secured, and the deed is delivered or placed in escrow). If the consummation criteria have not been satisfied, the seller uses the deposit method of accounting until all of the criteria are met (i.e., the sale has been consummated).

Adequacy of the Buyer's Initial Investment

Once the sale is consummated, the next step is to determine whether the buyer's initial investment adequately demonstrates a commitment to pay for the property and the reasonable likelihood that the seller will collect it. This determination is made by comparing the buyer's initial investment to the sales value of the property. In order to make the determination of whether the initial investment is adequate, the sales value of the property must also be computed.

Computation of Sales Value

The sales value of property in a real estate transaction is computed as follows:

	Stated sales price
+	Proceeds from the issuance of an exercised purchase option
+	Other payments that are, in substance, additional sales proceeds (e.g., management fees, points, prepaid interest, or fees required to be maintained in advance of the sale that will be applied against amounts due to the seller at a later point)
−	A discount that reduces the buyer's note to its present value
−	Net present value of services seller agrees to perform without compensation
−	Excess of net present value of services seller performs over compensation that seller will receive
=	Sales value of the property

Composition of the Initial Investment

Sales transactions are characterized by many different types of payments and commitments made among the seller, buyer, and third parties; however, the buyer's initial investment includes only the following:

1. Cash paid to the seller as a down payment.
2. Buyer's notes given to the seller that are supported by irrevocable letters of credit from independent lending institutions.
3. Payments by the buyer to third parties that reduce existing indebtedness the seller has on the property.
4. Other amounts paid by the buyer that are part of the sales value.
5. Other consideration received by the seller that can be converted to cash without recourse to the seller; for example, other notes of the buyer.

The following items are not included as initial investment:

1. Payments by the buyer to third parties for improvements to the property.
2. A permanent loan commitment by an independent third party to replace a loan made by the seller.
3. Funds that have been or will be loaned, refunded, or directly or indirectly provided to the buyer by the seller or loans guaranteed or collateralized by the seller for the buyer.

Size of Initial Investment

Once the initial investment is computed, its size must be compared to the sales value of the property. To qualify as an adequate initial investment, the initial investment must be equal to at least a major part of the difference between usual loan limits established by independent lending institutions and the sales value of the property. The minimum initial investment requirements for real estate sales (other than retail land sales) vary depending upon the type of property being sold. The following table provides the limits for the various properties:

Type of property	*Minimum initial investment expressed as a percentage of sales value*
Land	
Held for commercial, industrial, or residential development to commence within two years after sale	20
Held for commercial, industrial, or residential development to commence more than two years after sale	25
Commercial and Industrial Property	
Office and industrial buildings, shopping centers, and so forth:	
Properties subject to lease on a long-term lease basis to parties with satisfactory credit rating; cash flow currently sufficient to service all indebtedness	10
Single-tenancy properties sold to a buyer with a satisfactory credit rating	15
All other	20
Other income-producing properties (hotels, motels, marinas, mobile home parks, and so forth):	
Cash flow currently sufficient to service all indebtedness	15
Start-up situations or current deficiencies in cash flow	25
Multifamily Residential Property	
Primary residence:	
Cash flow currently sufficient to service all indebtedness	10
Start-up situations or current deficiencies in cash flow	15
Secondary or recreational residence:	
Cash flow currently sufficient to service all indebtedness	15
Start-up situations or current deficiencies in cash flow	25

Type of property	*Minimum initial investment expressed as a percentage of sales value*
Single-Family Residential Property (including condominium or cooperative housing)	
Primary residence of the buyer	5[a]
Secondary or recreational residence	10[a]

[a] *If collectibility of the remaining portion of the sales price cannot be supported by reliable evidence of collection experience, the minimum initial investment [is to] be at least 60% of the difference between the sales value and the financing available from loans guaranteed by regulatory bodies such as the Federal Housing Authority (FHA) or the Veterans Administration (VA), or from independent, established lending institutions. This 60% test applies when independent first-mortgage financing is not utilized and the seller takes a receivable from the buyer for the difference between the sales value and the initial investment. If independent first mortgage financing is utilized, the adequacy of the initial investment on sales of single-family residential property [is] determined [as described in the next paragraph].*

Lenders' appraisals of specific properties often differ. Therefore, if the buyer has obtained a permanent loan or firm permanent loan commitment for maximum financing of the property from an independent lending institution, the minimum initial investment must be the greater of the following:

1. The minimum percentage of the sales value of the property specified in the above table or
2. The lesser of

   a. The amount of the sales value of the property in excess of 115% of the amount of a newly placed permanent loan or firm loan commitment from a primary lender that is an independent established lending institution or
   b. 25% of the sales value

To illustrate the determination of whether an initial investment adequately demonstrates a commitment to pay for property, consider the following example:

Example determining adequacy of initial investment

Marcus, Inc. exercised a $2,000 option for the purchase of an apartment building from Rubin, Inc. The terms of the sales contract required Marcus to pay $3,000 of delinquent property taxes, pay a $300,000 cash down payment, assume Rubin's recently issued first mortgage of $1,200,000, and give Rubin a second mortgage of $500,000 at a prevailing interest rate.

Step 1 — Compute the sales value of the property.

Payment of back taxes to reduce Rubin's liability to local municipality	$ 3,000
Proceeds from exercised option	2,000
Cash down payment	300,000
First mortgage assumed by Marcus	1,200,000
Second mortgage given to Rubin	500,000
Sales value of the apartment complex	$2,005,000

Step 2 — Compute the initial investment.

Cash down payment	$ 300,000
Payment of back taxes to reduce Rubin's liability to local municipality	3,000
Proceeds from exercised option	2,000
	$ 305,000

Step 3 — Compute the minimum initial investment required.

a. The minimum percentage of the sales value of the property as specified in the table is $200,500 ($2,005,000 × 10%).

b. 1. The amount of the sales value of the property in excess of 115% of the recently placed permanent mortgage is $625,000 (sales value of $2,005,000 − $1,380,000 [= 115% of $1,200,000]).

   2. 25% of the sales value ($2,005,000) is $501,250.

The lesser of b.1. and b.2. is b.2., $501,250. The greater of a. and b. is b., $501,250. Therefore, to record this transaction under the full accrual method (assuming all other criteria are met), the minimum initial investment must be equal to or greater than $501,250. Since the actual initial investment is only $305,000, all or part of the recognition of profit from the transaction must be postponed.

If the sale has been consummated but the buyer's initial investment does not adequately demonstrate a commitment to pay, the transaction is accounted for using the installment method when the seller is reasonably assured of recovering the cost of the property if the buyer defaults. However, if the recovery of the cost of the property is not reasonably assured should the buyer default or if the cost has been recovered and the collection of additional amounts is uncertain, the cost recovery or deposit method is used.

Adequacy of the Buyer's Continuing Investments

The collectibility of the buyer's receivable must be reasonably assured; therefore, for full profit recognition under the full accrual method, the buyer must be contractually required to pay each year on its total debt for the purchase price of the property an amount at least equal to the level annual payment that would be needed to pay that debt (both principal and interest) over a specified period. This period is no more than 20 years for land, and no more than the customary amortization term of a first mortgage loan by an independent lender for other types of real estate. For continuing investment purposes, the contractually required payments must be in a form that is acceptable for an initial investment. If the seller provides funds to the buyer, either directly or indirectly, these funds must be subtracted from the buyer's payments in determining whether the continuing investments are adequate.

The indebtedness on the property does not have to be reduced proportionately. A lump-sum (balloon) payment will not affect the amortization of the receivable as long as the level annual payments still meet the minimum annual amortization requirement. For example, a land real estate sale may require the buyer to make level annual payments at the end of each of the first five years and then a balloon payment at the end of the sixth year. The continuing investment criterion is met provided the level annual payment required in each of the first 5 years is greater than or equal to the level annual payment that would be made if the receivable were amortized over the maximum 20-year (land's specified term) period.

Continuing Investment Not Qualifying

If the sale has been consummated and the minimum initial investment criteria have been satisfied but the continuing investment by the buyer does not meet the stated criterion, the seller recognizes profit by the reduced profit method at the time of sale if payments by the buyer each year will at least cover both of the following:

1. The interest and principal amortization on the maximum first mortgage loan that could be obtained on the property.
2. Interest, at an appropriate rate, on the excess of the aggregate actual debt on the property over such a maximum first mortgage loan.

If the payments by the buyer do not cover both of the above, the seller recognizes profit by either the installment or cost recovery method.

Release Provisions

An agreement to sell real estate may provide that part or all of the property sold will be released from liens by payment of an amount sufficient to release the debt or by an assignment of the buyer's payments until release. In order to meet the criteria of an adequate initial investment, the investment must be sufficient both to pay the release on property released and to meet the initial investment requirements on property not released. If not, profit is recognized on each released portion as if it were a separate sale when a sale has been deemed to have taken place.

Seller's Receivable Subject to Future Subordination

The seller's receivable should not be subject to future subordination. Future subordination by a primary lender would permit the lender to obtain a lien on the property, giving the seller only a secondary residual claim. This subordination criterion does not apply if either of the following occur:

1. A receivable is subordinate to a first mortgage on the property existing at the time of sale.
2. A future loan, including an existing permanent loan commitment, is provided for by the terms of the sale and the proceeds of the loan will be applied first to the payment of the seller's receivable.

If the seller's receivable is subject to future subordination, profit is recognized using the cost recovery method. The cost recovery method is justified because the collectibility of the sales price is not reasonably assured in circumstances when the receivable may be subordinated to amounts due to other creditors.

Seller's Continuing Involvement

Sometimes sellers continue to be involved with property for periods of time even though the property has been legally sold. The seller's involvement often takes the form of profit participation, management services, financing, guarantees of return, construction, and so on. The seller does not have a substantial continuing involvement with property unless the risks and rewards of ownership have been clearly transferred to the buyer.

If the seller has some continuing involvement with the property and does not clearly transfer substantially all of the risks and rewards of ownership, profit is recognized by a method other than the full accrual method. The method chosen is determined by the nature and extent of the seller's continuing involvement. As a general rule, profit is recognized at the time of sale only if the amount of the seller's loss due to the continued involvement with the property is limited by the terms of the sales contract. In this event, the profit recognized at this time is reduced by the maximum possible loss from the continued involvement.

When investors create a jointly owned entity, the arrangement may include a buy-sell clause that gives both investors the ability to offer to buy the other investor's interest in the entity. When an investor makes a purchase offer under this clause, the recipient of the offer can sell its interest for the offered amount or buy the other party's interest at the same price. A buy-sell clause does not necessarily constitute a prohibited form of continuing involvement that would preclude partial sales treatment. However, it should be evaluated to see if it essentially gives the buyer an in-substance option to put its interest in the entity back to the seller or gives the seller an in-substance option to acquire the buyer's interest in the entity. If so, the buy-sell clause is a prohibited form of continuing involvement that precludes profit recognition.

Profit-Sharing, Financing, and Leasing Arrangements

In real estate sales, it is often the case that economic substance takes precedence over legal form. Certain transactions, though possibly called sales, are in substance profit-sharing, financing, or leasing arrangements and are accounted for as such. These include situations in which

1. The seller has an obligation to repurchase the property, or the terms of the transaction allow the buyer to compel the seller to repurchase the property or give the seller an option to do so.
2. The seller is a general partner in a limited partnership that acquires an interest in the property sold and holds a receivable from the buyer for a significant part (15% of the maximum first-lien financing) of the sales price.
3. The seller guarantees the return of the buyer's investment or a return on that investment for an extended period of time.
4. The seller is required to initiate or support operations, or continue to operate the property at its own risk for an extended period of time.

Options to Purchase Real Estate Property

Often a buyer will buy an option to purchase land from a seller with the hopeful intention of obtaining a zoning change, building permit, or some other contingency specified in the option agreement. Proceeds from the issue of an option by a property owner (seller) are accounted for by the deposit method. If the option is exercised, the seller includes the option proceeds in the computation of the sales value of the property. If the option is not exercised, the seller recognizes the option proceeds as income at the time the option expires.

Partial Sales of Property

A sale is a partial sale if the seller retains an equity interest in the property or has an equity interest in the buyer. Profit on a partial sale may be recognized on the date of sale if the following occur:

1. The buyer is independent of the seller.
2. Collection of the sales price is reasonably assured.
3. The seller will not be required to support the operations of the property on its related obligations to an extent greater than its proportionate interest.

If the buyer is not independent of the seller, the seller may not be able to recognize any profit that is measured at the date of sale.

If the seller is not reasonably assured of collecting the sales price, the cost recovery or installment method is used to recognize profit on the partial sale.

A seller who separately sells individual units in condominium projects or time-sharing interests recognizes profit by the percentage-of-completion method on the sale of individual units or interests if all of the following five criteria are met:

1. Construction is beyond a preliminary stage (i.e., engineering and design work, execution of construction contracts, site clearance and preparation, excavation, and the building foundation have all been completed).
2. The buyer is unable to obtain a refund except for nondelivery of the units or interest.
3. Sufficient units have been sold to assure that the entire property will not revert to being rental property.
4. Sales prices are collectible.
5. Aggregate sales proceeds and costs can be reasonably estimated.

The deposit method is used to account for these sales up to the point all the criteria are met for recognition of a sale.

Selection of Method

If a loss is apparent (e.g., the carrying value of the property exceeds the sum of the deposit, fair value of unrecorded note receivable, and the debt assumed by the buyer), then immediate recognition of the loss is required.

The installment method is used if the full accrual method cannot be used due to an inadequate initial investment by the buyer, provided that recovery of cost is reasonably assured if the buyer defaults. The cost recovery method or the deposit method is used if such cost recovery is not assured.

The reduced profit method is used when the buyer's initial investment is adequate but the continuing investment is not adequate, and payments by the buyer at least cover the sum of (1) the amortization (principal and interest) on the maximum first mortgage that could be obtained on the property and (2) the interest, at an appropriate rate, on the excess of aggregate debt over the maximum first mortgage.

METHODS OF ACCOUNTING FOR REAL ESTATE SALES OTHER THAN RETAIL LAND SALES

Full Accrual Method

This method of accounting for nonretail sales of real estate is appropriate when all four of the recognition criteria have been satisfied. The full accrual method is simply the application of the revenue recognition principle. A real estate sale is recognized in full when the profit is determinable and the earnings process is virtually complete. The profit is determinable when the first three criteria have been met (the sale is consummated, the buyer has demonstrated a commitment to pay, and the seller's receivable is not subject to future subordination). The earnings process is virtually complete when the fourth criterion has been met (the seller has transferred the risks and rewards of ownership and does not have a substantial continuing involvement with the property). If all of the criteria have not been met, the seller records the transaction by one of the following methods:

1. Deposit
2. Cost recovery
3. Installment
4. Reduced profit
5. Percentage-of-completion (see Chapter 7, Revenue Recognition for Long-Term Construction Contracts)

Profit under the full accrual method is computed by subtracting the cost basis of the property surrendered from the sales value given by the buyer. Also, the computation of profit on the sale includes all costs incurred that are directly related to the sale, such as accounting and legal fees.

Installment Method

Under the installment method, each cash receipt and principal payment by the buyer on debt assumed with recourse to the seller consists of part recovery of cost and part recovery of profit. The apportionment between cost recovery and profit is in the same ratio as total cost and total profit bear to the sales value of the property sold. Therefore, under the installment method, the seller recognizes profit on each payment that the buyer makes to the seller and on each payment the buyer makes to the holder of the primary debt. When a buyer assumes debt that is without recourse to the seller, the seller recognizes profit on each payment made to the seller and on the entire debt assumed by the buyer. The accounting treatment differs because the seller is subject to substantially different levels of risk under the alternative conditions. For debt that is without recourse, the seller recovers a portion, if not all, of the cost of the asset surrendered at the time the buyer assumes the debt.

Example of the installment method

Assume Tucker sells to Price a plot of undeveloped land for $2 million. Price will assume, with recourse, Tucker's existing first mortgage of $1 million and also pay Tucker a $300,000 cash down payment. Price will pay the balance of $700,000 by giving Tucker a second mortgage payable in equal installments of principal and interest over a ten-year period. The cost of the land to Tucker was $1.2 million, and Price will commence development of the land immediately.

1. Computation of sales value:

Cash down payment	$ 300,000
First mortgage	1,000,000
Second mortgage	700,000
Sales value	$2,000,000

2. Computation of the initial investment:

Cash down payment	$ 300,000

3. Computation of the minimum required initial investment:
    a. $400,000 ($2,000,000 × 20%)
    b. 1. $850,000 [$2,000,000 − (115% × 1,000,000)]
       2. $500,000 ($2,000,000 × 25%)

The minimum initial investment is $500,000 since b.2. is less than b.1. and b.2. is greater than a.

The initial investment criterion has not been satisfied because the actual initial investment is less than the minimum initial investment. Therefore, assuming the sale has been consummated and Tucker is reasonably assured of recovering the cost of the land from Price, the installment method is to be used. The gross profit to be recognized over the installment payment period by Tucker is computed as follows:

Sales value	$ 2,000,000
Cost of land	(1,200,000)
Gross profit	$ 800,000

The gross profit percentage to apply to each payment by Price to Tucker and the primary debt holder is 40% ($800,000 / $2,000,000).

If Price also pays $50,000 of principal on the first mortgage and $70,000 of principal on the second mortgage in the year of sale, Tucker would recognize the following profit in the year of sale:

Profit recognized on the down payment ($300,000 × 40%)	$120,000
Profit recognized on the principal payments:	
First mortgage ($50,000 × 40%)	20,000
Second mortgage ($70,000 × 40%)	28,000
Total profit recognized in year of sale	$168,000

Note that Tucker recognizes profit only on the payment applicable to the first mortgage. This is because Tucker may be called upon to satisfy the liability on the first mortgage if Price defaults.

If Tucker's first mortgage was assumed without recourse, Tucker would recognize the following profit in the year of sale:

Profit recognized on the down payment ($300,000 × 40%)	$120,000
Profit recognized on Price's assumption of Tucker's first mortgage without recourse ($1,000,000 × 40%)	400,000
Profit recognized on the principal payment of the second mortgage ($70,000 × 40%)	28,000
Total profit recognized in year of sale	$548,000

The income statement (or related footnotes) for the period of sale includes the sales value received, the gross profit recognized, the gross profit deferred, and the costs of sale. In future periods when further payments are made to the buyer, the seller realizes gross profit on these payments. This amount is presented as a single line item in the revenue section of the income statement.

If, in the future, the transaction meets the requirements for the full accrual method of recognizing profit, the seller may change to that method and recognize the remaining deferred profit as income at that time.

Cost Recovery Method

When the cost recovery method is used (e.g., when the seller's receivable is subject to subordination or the seller is not reasonably assured of recovering the cost of the property if the buyer defaults), no profit is recognized on the sales transaction until the seller has recovered the cost of the property sold. If the buyer assumes debt that is with recourse to the seller, profit is not recognized by the seller until the cash payments by the buyer, including both principal and interest on debt due the seller and on debt assumed by the buyer, exceed the seller's cost of the property sold. If the buyer assumes debt that is without recourse to the seller, profit may be recognized by the seller when the cash payments by the buyer, including both principal and interest on debt due the seller, exceed the difference between the seller's cost of the property and the nonrecourse debt assumed by the buyer.

For the cost recovery method, principal collections reduce the seller's related receivable, and interest collections on such receivable increase the deferred gross profit on the balance sheet.

Example of the cost recovery method

Assume that on January 1, 2010, Simon, Inc. purchased undeveloped land with a sales value of $365,000 from Davis Co. The sales value is represented by a $15,000 cash down payment, Simon assuming Davis's $200,000 first mortgage (10%, payable in equal annual installments over the next 20 years), and Simon giving Davis a second mortgage of $150,000 (12%, payable in equal annual installments over the next 10 years). The sale has been consummated, but the initial investment is below the minimum required amount and Davis is not reasonably assured of recovering the cost of the property if Simon defaults. The cost of the land to Davis was $300,000. The circumstances indicate the cost recovery method is appropriate. The transaction is recorded by Davis as follows:

1/1/11	Notes receivable	150,000	
	First mortgage payable	200,000	
	Cash	15,000	
	Revenue from sale of land		365,000
	Revenue from sale of land	365,000	
	Land		300,000
	Deferred gross profit		65,000

Case 1: The first mortgage was assumed with recourse to Davis. Immediately after the sale, the unrecovered cost of the land is computed as follows:

Land	$300,000
Less: Cash down payment	(15,000)
Unrecovered cost	$285,000

The note (second mortgage) is reported as follows:

Note receivable	$150,000	
Less: Deferred gross profit	(65,000)	$ 85,000

At the end of the year Simon pays $26,547.64 ($8,547.64 principal and $18,000.00 interest) on the second mortgage note and $23,491.94 ($3,491.94 principal and $20,000.00 interest) on the first mortgage. At 12/31/11 the unrecovered cost of the land is computed as follows:

Previous unrecovered cost		$285,000.00
Less: Note receivable payment	$26,547.64	
First mortgage payment	23,491.94	(50,039.58)
Unrecovered cost		$234,960.42

The receivable is reported on the 12/31/11 balance sheet as follows:

Note receivable ($150,000 – 8,547.64) $141,452.36
Less: Deferred gross profit ($65,000 +
    18,000)   <u>83,000.00</u> $58,452.36

Case 2:   The first mortgage is assumed without recourse to Davis. The reporting of the note is the same as Case 1; however, the unrecovered cost of the property is different. Immediately after the sale, the unrecovered cost of the property is computed as follows:

Land	$300,000
Less: Cash down payment	(15,000)
Nonrecourse debt assumed by	
Simon	<u>(200,000)</u>
Unrecovered cost	$ <u>85,000</u>

After Simon makes the payments at the end of the year, the unrecovered cost is computed as follows:

Previous unrecovered cost	$85,000.00
Less: Notes receivable payment	<u>26,547.64</u>
Unrecovered cost	$<u>58,452.36</u>

For the cost recovery method, the income statement for the year the real estate sale occurs includes the sales value received, the cost of the property given up, and the gross profit deferred. In future periods, after the cost of the property has been recovered, the income statement includes the gross profit earned as a separate revenue item.

If, after accounting for the sale by the cost recovery method, circumstances indicate that the criteria for the full accrual method are satisfied, the seller may change to the full accrual method and recognize any remaining deferred gross profit in full.

Deposit Method

When the deposit method is used (e.g., when the sale is, in substance, the sale of an option and not real estate), the seller does not recognize any profit, does not record a receivable, continues to report in its financial statements the property and the related existing debt even if the debt has been assumed by the buyer, and discloses that those items are subject to a sales contract. The seller also continues to recognize depreciation expense on the property for which the deposits have been received, unless the property has been classified as held for sale. Cash received from the buyer (initial and continuing investments) is reported as a deposit on the contract. However, some amounts of cash may be received that are not subject to refund, such as interest on the unrecorded principal. These amounts are used to offset any carrying charges on the property (e.g., property taxes and interest on the existing debt). If the interest collected on the unrecorded receivable is refundable, the seller records this interest as a deposit before the sale is consummated and then includes it as a part of the initial investment once the sale is consummated. If deposits on retail land sales are eventually recognized as sales, the interest portion of the deposit is separately recognized as interest income. For contracts that are cancelled, the nonrefundable amounts are recognized as income and the refundable amounts returned to the depositor at the time of cancellation.

As stated, the seller's balance sheet continues to present the debt assumed by the buyer (this includes nonrecourse debt) among its other liabilities. However, the seller reports any principal payments on the mortgage debt assumed as additional deposits, while correspondingly reducing the carrying amount of the mortgage debt.

Example of a deposit transaction

Elbrus Investments enters into two separate property acquisition transactions with the Buena Vista Land Company.

1. Elbrus pays a $50,000 deposit and promises to pay an additional $800,000 to buy land and a building in an area not yet properly zoned for the facility Elbrus intends to construct. Final acquisition of the property is contingent upon these zoning changes. Buena Vista does not record the receivable, and records the deposit with the following entry:

Cash	50,000	
Customer deposits		50,000

   Part of the purchase agreement stipulates that Buena Vista will retain all interest earned on the deposit, and that 10% of the deposit is nonrefundable. Buena Vista earns 5% interest on Elbrus's deposit over a period of four months, resulting in $208 of interest income that is offset against the property tax expenses of the property with the following entry:

Cash	208	
Property tax expense		208

   Immediately thereafter, the required zoning changes are turned down, and Elbrus cancels the sales contract. Buena Vista returns the refundable portion of the deposit to Elbrus and records the nonrefundable portion as income with the following entry:

Customer deposits	50,000	
Income from contract cancellation		10,000
Cash		40,000

2. Elbrus pays a $40,000 deposit on land owned and being improved by Buena Vista. Elbrus immediately begins paying $5,000/month under a four-year, 7% loan agreement totaling $212,000 of principal payments, and agrees to pay an additional $350,000 at closing, subject to the land being approved for residential construction. After two

months, Buena Vista has earned $167 of refundable interest income on Elbrus's deposit and has been paid $7,689 of refundable principal and $2,311 of refundable interest on the debt. Buena Vista records these events with the following entry:

Cash	10,167	
Customer deposits		10,167

The land is approved for residential construction, triggering sale of the property. Buena Vista's basis in the property is $520,000. Buena Vista uses the following entry to describe completion of the sale:

Cash	350,000	
Note receivable	204,311	
Customer deposits	50,167	
Gain on asset sale		84,478
Land		520,000

Reduced Profit Method

The reduced profit method is appropriate when the sale has been consummated and the initial investment is adequate but the continuing investment does not clearly demonstrate the buyer's willing commitment to pay the remaining balance of the receivable. For example, a buyer may purchase land under an agreement in which the seller will finance the sale over a 30-year period. Twenty years is the maximum amortization period for the purchase of land; therefore, the agreement fails to meet the continuing investment criteria.

Under the reduced profit method, the seller recognizes a portion of the profit at the time of sale with the remaining portion recognized in future periods. The amount of reduced profit recognized at the time of sale is determined by discounting the receivable from the buyer to the present value of the lowest level of annual payments required by the sales contract over the maximum period of time specified for that type of real estate property (twenty years for land and the customary term of a first mortgage loan set by an independent lending institution for other types of real estate). The remaining profit is recognized in the periods that lump-sum or other payments are made.

Example of the reduced profit method

Assume Levinson, Inc. sells a parcel of land to Raemer Co. Levinson receives sales value of $2 million. The land cost $1.6 million. Raemer gave Levinson the following consideration:

Cash down payment	$ 500,000
First mortgage note payable to an independent lending institution (payable in equal installments of principal and 12% interest, $133,887 payable at the end of each of the next 20 years)	1,000,000
Second mortgage note payable to Levinson (payable in equal installments of principal and 10% interest, $53,039 payable at the end of each of the next 30 years)	500,000
Total sales value	$2,000,000

The amortization term of the second mortgage (seller's receivable) exceeds the twenty-year maximum. It is assumed that the payments by the buyer will cover the interest and principal on the maximum first mortgage loan that could be obtained on the property and interest on the excess aggregate debt on the property over such a maximum first mortgage loan; consequently, the reduced profit method is appropriate. It is also assumed that the market interest rate on similar agreements is 14%.

The present value of $53,039 per year for 20 years at the market rate of 14% is $351,278 ($53,039 × 6.623).

The gross profit on the sale ($400,000) is reduced by the difference between the face amount of the seller's receivable ($500,000) and the reduced amount ($351,278) or $148,722. The profit recognized at the time of sale is the sales value less the cost of the land less the difference between the face amount of the receivable and the reduced amount. Therefore, the reduced profit recognized on the date of sale is computed as follows:

Sales value	$2,000,000
Less: Cost of land	(1,600,000)
Excess	(148,722)
Reduced profit	$ 251,278

Under the reduced profit method, the seller amortizes its receivable at the market rate, not the rate given on the second mortgage. The receivable's carrying balance is zero after the specified term expires (in this case, 20 years). The remaining profit of $148,722 is recognized in the years after the specified term expires as the buyer makes payments on the second mortgage (years 21 through 30).

PROFIT RECOGNITION ON RETAIL LAND SALES

A single method of recognizing profit is applied to all consummated sales transactions within a project.

Full Accrual Method

The full accrual method of accounting is applied if all of the following conditions are met and a sale can be recorded:

1. **Expiration of refund period.** The buyer has made the down payment and each required subsequent payment until the period of

cancellation with refund has expired. That period is the longest period of those required by local law, established by the seller's policy, or specified in the contract.

2. **Sufficient cumulative payments.** The cumulative payments of
   principal and interest equal or exceed 10% of the contract sales
   price.

3. **Collectibility of receivables.** Collection experience for the project
   in which the sale is made or for the seller's prior projects indicates
   that at least 90% of the contracts in the project in which the sale is
   made that are in force six months after sale will be collected in full.
   The collection experience with the seller's prior projects may be
   applied to a new project if the prior projects have

   a. The same characteristics (type of land, environment, clientele,
      contract terms, sales methods) as the new project
   b. A sufficiently long collection period to indicate the percentage
      of current sales of the new project that will be collected to ma-
      turity

   A down payment of at least 20% is an acceptable indication of
   collectibility.

4. **Nonsubordination of receivables.** The receivable from the sale is
   not subject to subordination to new loans on the property except
   that subordination by an individual lot buyer for home construction
   purposes is permissible if the collection experience on those contracts is the same as on contracts not subordinated.

5. **Completion of development.** The seller is not obligated to complete improvements of lots sold or to construct amenities or other
   facilities applicable to lots sold.

Percentage-of-Completion Method

The percentage-of-completion method is used if criteria 1., 2., 3.,
and 4. are met, and full accrual criteria are not met (criterion 5 is not satisfied). However, additional criteria (6. and 7.) must be satisfied.

6. **There has been progress on improvements.** The project's improvements progressed beyond preliminary stages and the work
   apparently will be completed according to plan. Some indications
   of progress are

   a. The expenditure of funds
   b. Initiation of work
   c. Existence of engineering plans and work commitments
   d. Completion of access roads and amenities such as golf courses,
      clubs, and swimming pools

Additionally, there should be no indication of significant delaying factors, such as the inability to obtain permits, contractors, personnel, or equipment. Finally, estimates of costs to complete and extent of progress toward completion should be reasonably dependable.

7. **Development is practical.** There is an expectation that the land can be developed for the purposes represented and the properties will be useful for those purposes; restrictions, including environmental restrictions, will not seriously hamper development; and that improvements such as access roads, water supply, and sewage treatment or removal are feasible within a reasonable time period.

Installment Method

The installment method is appropriate if criteria a. and b. are met, full accrual criteria are not met, and the seller is financially capable, as shown by capital structure, cash flow, or borrowing capacity. If the transaction subsequently meets the requirements for the full accrual method, the seller is permitted to change to that method. This would be a change in accounting estimate. This method may be changed to the percentage-of-completion method when all of the criteria are met.

Deposit Method

If a retail land sale transaction does not meet any of the above criteria, the deposit method is appropriate.

TIME-SHARE TRANSACTIONS

A major segment of the real estate industry has evolved in recent decades to market and sell time-shares, whereby parties acquire the right to use property (typically, resort condominiums or other vacation-oriented property) for a fixed number of weeks per year (known as intervals). While a vast variety of property types and transaction structures exist, there are certain common features and complexities that have challenged the accounting profession. Time-sharing transactions are characterized by the following:

1. Volume-based, homogeneous sales
2. Seller financing
3. Relatively high selling and marketing costs
4. Upon default, recovery of the time-sharing interval by the seller and some forfeiture of principal by the buyer

Profit recognition. A time-share seller should recognize profit on time-sharing transactions. In order to justify recognizing profit, nonreversionary title must be transferred. If title transfer is reversionary, on the other hand, the seller must account for the transaction as if it were an operating lease.

For a time-sharing transaction to be accounted for as a sale, it must meet the following criteria:

1. The seller transfers nonreversionary title to the time-share.
2. The transaction is *consummated*.
3. The buyer makes cumulative payments (excluding interest) of at least 10% of the sales value of the time-share.
4. Sufficient time-shares would have been sold to reasonably assure that the units will not become rental property.

Effect of sales incentives. Certain sales incentives provided by a seller to a buyer to consummate a transaction are to be recorded separately, by reducing the stated sales price of the time-share by the excess of the fair value of the incentive over the amount paid by the buyer. For purposes of testing for buyer's financial commitment, the seller must reduce its measurement of the buyer's initial and continuing investments by the excess of the fair value of the incentive over the stated amount the buyer pays, except in certain situations in which the buyer is required to make specific payments on its note in order to receive the incentive.

Reload transactions. A reload transaction is considered to be a separate sale of a second interval. For an upgrade transaction, that guidance is applied to the sales value of the new (upgrade) interval, and the buyer's initial and continuing investments from the original interval are included in the profit recognition tests related to the new interval.

Uncollectibles. The term *uncollectibles* includes all situations in which, as a result of credit issues, a time-share seller collects less than 100% of the contractual cash payments of a note receivable, except for certain transfers of receivables to independent third parties by the seller. An estimate of uncollectibility that is expected to occur should be recorded as a reduction of revenue at the time that profit is recognized on a time-sharing sale recorded under the full accrual or percentage-of-completion method. Historical and statistical perspectives are used in making such a determination of anticipated uncollectible amounts. Subsequent changes in estimated uncollectibles should be recorded as an adjustment to estimated uncollectibles and thereby as an adjustment to revenue. Under the relative sales value method, the seller effectively does not record revenue, cost of sales, or inventory relief for amounts not expected to be collected. There generally is no accounting effect on inventory when, as expected, a time-share is repossessed or otherwise reacquired.

Cost of sales. The seller should account for cost of sales and time-sharing inventory in accordance with the relative sales value method.

Costs charged to current period expense. All costs incurred to sell time-shares would be charged to expense as incurred except for certain costs that are

- Incurred for tangible assets used directly in selling the time-shares;
- Incurred for services performed to obtain regulatory approval of sales; or
- Direct and incremental costs of successful sales efforts under the percentage-of-completion, installment, reduced profit, or deposit methods of accounting.

Incidental operations. Rental and other operations during holding periods, including sampler programs and minivacations, should be accounted for as incidental operations. This requires that any excess of revenue over costs be recorded as a reduction of inventory costs.

SPEs and other complex structures. The accounting treatment for more complex time-sharing structures such as time-sharing SPEs, points systems, and vacation clubs should be determined using the same profit recognition guidance as for simpler structures, provided that the time-sharing interest has been sold to the end user. For balance sheet presentation purposes, an SPE should be viewed as an entity lacking economic substance and established for the purpose of facilitating sales if the SPE structure is legally required for purposes of selling intervals to a class of nonresident customers, and the SPE has no assets other than the time-sharing intervals and has no debt. In those circumstances, the seller should present on its balance sheet as time-sharing inventory the interests in the SPE not yet sold to end users.

Continuing involvement by seller or related entities. If the seller, seller's affiliate, or related party operates an exchange, points, affinity, or similar program, the program's operations constitute continuing involvement by the seller, and the seller should determine its accounting based on an evaluation of whether it will receive compensation at prevailing market rates for its program services.

OTHER ISSUES RELATED TO REAL ESTATE SALES TRANSACTIONS

Sales of Integral Equipment

Sales of integral equipment are part of a real estate sale, and thus the determination of whether equipment is integral is an important one. A determination of whether equipment to be leased is integral is also necessary to enable lessors to determine the proper accounting for sales-type leases. This determination is to be made based on two factors. The first is the significance of the cost to remove the equipment from its existing location (which would include any costs of repairing the damage done to that location by the act of removal). The second is the decrease in value of the equipment that results from its removal (which is, at a minimum, the cost to ship and reinstall the equipment at a new site). The nature of the equipment and whether others can use it is considered in determining whether there would be any further diminution in fair value. When the combined total of the cost to remove and any further diminution of value exceeds 10% of the fair value of the equipment (installed), the equipment is to be deemed integral equipment.

Valuation Allowance Carryforward

A valuation allowance may be previously established for a loan that is collateralized by a long-lived asset. Should it be carried forward after the asset is foreclosed due to loan default? When such a loan is foreclosed, any valuation allowance established for the foreclosed loan should not be carried over as a separate element of the cost basis for purposes of accounting for the long-lived assets. Rather, upon foreclosure, the lender must measure the long-lived asset received in full satisfaction of a receivable at fair value less cost to sell. This results in the identification of a new cost basis for the long-lived asset received in full satisfaction of a receivable.

Impaired Asset Value Recovery

An impaired asset obtained by means of foreclosure may later recover some value. In this case, a gain shall be recognized for any subsequent increase in fair value less cost to sell, but not in excess of the cumulative loss previously recognized (for a write-down to fair value less cost to sell). Thus, gain recognition is limited to the cumulative extent that losses have been recognized while the assets were accounted for as long-lived assets. "Recovery" of losses not recognized is thus not permitted.

Graduated Payment Mortgages

Graduated payment mortgages for which negative principal amortization is recognized do not meet the continuing investment tests, and thus full profit is not to be recognized immediately.

Mortgage Insurance Equivalency

Mortgage insurance is not to be considered the equivalent of an irrevocable letter of credit in determining whether profit is to be recognized, and the purchase of such insurance is not in itself a demonstration of commitment by the buyer to honor its obligation to pay for the property. The sole exception to this rule is that for all FHA (Federal Housing Administration) and VA (Veteran's Administration) insured loans, profits may be recognized under the full accrual method.

Antispeculation Clauses

Antispeculation clauses are sometimes found in land sale agreements, requiring the buyer to develop the land in a specific manner or within a specific period of time and giving the seller the right, but not the obligation, to reacquire the property when the condition is not met. This option does not preclude recognition of a sale if the probability of the buyer not complying is remote.

Financing Impact on Profit Recognition

There are a range of possible forms of financing, each having a unique impact on profit recognition. The following guidelines are to be used by a seller of real estate:

1. In determining whether a transaction qualifies for accounting using the full accrual method of profit recognition, initial and continuing investment requirements must be considered unless the seller has unconditionally received all amounts due and is not at risk related to the financing.
2. In determining the buyer's initial investment, payments made on debt incurred by the buyer that is secured by the property (irrespective of whether the debt are incurred directly from the seller or other parties or indirectly by assumption) are not part of the initial investment. Also excluded from the initial investment are payments made to the seller out of the proceeds from debt described in the preceding sentence.
3. Under the installment method, cost recovery method, and reduced-profit recognition methods, payments described in item 2. are not considered to be cash payments from the buyer. If, however, the

deferred profit exceeds the sum of (a) the outstanding amount of seller financing, and (b) the outstanding amount of the buyer's debt secured by the property for which the seller is contingently liable, the excess amount is recognized as income by the seller.

Repossessed Real Estate Valuation

Repossessed real estate may be recorded at the lower of the net receivable due to the seller at foreclosure or the fair value of the property. After foreclosure, foreclosed assets are carried at the lower of fair value (less costs to sell) or cost.

REIT Minority Interests

The net equity of the operating partnership (after the contributions of the sponsor and the REIT) multiplied by the sponsor's ownership percentage in the operating partnership represents the amount to be initially reported as the minority interest in the REIT's consolidated financial statements. If a minority interest balance is negative, the related charge in the REIT's income statement is the greater of the minority interest holder's share of current earnings or the amount of distributions to the minority interest holder during the year. Any excess is to be credited directly to equity until elimination of the minority interest deficit that existed at the formation of the REIT. Subsequent acquisitions by the REIT, for cash, of a sponsor's minority interest in an operating partnership are accounted for consistent with the accounting for formation of the REIT.

Commitment Fees

Ccommitment fees are to be amortized over the combined commitment and loan period.

Investments in Real Estate Ventures

Owners of real estate ventures should generally use the equity method of accounting to account for their investments. However, limited partners may have such a minor interest and have no influence or control, in which case the cost method would instead be appropriate.

If losses exceed the investment, the losses are to be recognized regardless of any increase in the estimated fair value of the venture's assets. Losses in excess of the amount of the investment are a liability. Losses that cannot be borne by certain investors require the remaining investors to determine their share of any additional loss. Limited partners are not required to record losses in excess of their investment. As usual, if investors do not recognize losses in excess of investment, the equity method is resumed only after the investor's share of net income exceeds the cumulative net losses not recognized previously.

Venture agreements may designate different allocations for profits, losses, cash distributions and cash from liquidation. Accounting for equity in profits and losses therefore requires consideration of allocation formulas because the substance over form concept requires equity method accounting to follow the ultimate cash allocations.

Contributions of real estate to a venture as capital are recorded by the investor at cost, and cannot result in the recognition of a gain, since a capital contribution does not represent the culmination of the earnings process.

Interest on loans and advances that are, in substance, capital contributions and so are accounted for as distributions and not interest.

Real Estate Syndication Fees

All fees charged by syndicators are includable in the determination of sales value, except for syndication fees and fees for which future services must be performed. Syndication fees are recognized as income when the earning process is complete and collectibility is reasonably assured. If fees are unreasonable, they are to be adjusted, and the sales price of the real estate is to be appropriately adjusted as well. If a partnership interest is received by the syndicator, the value is included in the test of fee reasonableness. If it is part of the fee, the syndicators are to account for this interest as a retained interest from the partial sale of real estate. Fees for future services are recognized when the service is rendered.

Fees received from blind pool transactions are recognized ratably as the syndication partnership invests in property but only to the extent that the fees are nonrefundable. If syndicators are exposed to future losses from material involvement or from uncertainties regarding collectibility, income is deferred until the losses can be reasonably estimated. For purposes of determining the buyer's initial and continuing investment for profit recognition, before cash received by syndicators can be allocated to initial and continuing investment, it is allocated to (1) unpaid syndication fees until such fees are paid in full, and (2) amounts previously allocated to fees for future services (to the extent such services have already been performed when the cash is collected). If syndicators receive or retain partnership interests that are subordinated, these are accounted for as participations in future profits without risk of loss.

DISCLOSURES FOR REAL ESTATE SALES

In a sale-leaseback transaction, disclosure should be made of the terms of the transaction, including future commitments, obligations, provisions, or circumstances that either require or result in the seller's continuing involvement in the transaction. If the seller accounts for a sale-leaseback transaction under the deposit method or as a financing, disclosure should also be made of future minimum lease payments both in aggregate and for each of the following five years; the same reporting also applies to noncancelable sublease rentals. A sample disclosure follows:

> The Company finances a portion of its stores through sale-leaseback transactions. The properties are sold and the resulting leases qualify and are accounted for as operating leases. The Company does not have any retained or contingent interests in the stores, nor does the Company provide any guarantee, other than a guarantee of lease payments, in connection with the sale-leaseback transactions. Proceeds from the sale-leaseback transactions totaled $_____ in 2011, $_____ in 2010, and $_____ in 2009.

The seller of a time-share should disclose the maturities of notes receivable for each of the five following years and in aggregate for all years thereafter, as well as the weighted-average and range of stated interest rates of the notes. Disclosure should also include the estimated cost to complete improvements and promised amenities. An additional time-share disclosure is the activity in the allowance for uncollectible notes receivable, including the beginning balance, additions to the allowance account, write-offs, and changes in estimate associated with prior-period sales. A sample disclosure follows:

> The Company recognizes sales when (1) it has received a minimum of 10% of the purchase price for the timeshare interval, (2) the purchaser's period to cancel for a refund has expired, (3) the Company deems the receivables to be collectible, and (4) it has attained certain minimum sales and construction levels. The Company defers all revenue using the deposit method for sales that do not meet all four of these criteria. For sales that do not qualify for full revenue recognition as the project has progressed beyond the preliminary stages but has not yet reached completion, all revenue and profit are deferred and recognized in earnings using the percentage-of-completion method.

11 REVENUE RECOGNITION FOR RECORDING AND MUSIC

OVERVIEW

In the recording and music industry, business is transacted through license agreements, contractual arrangements entered into by an owner (licensor) of a music master or copyright. License agreements are modifications of the compulsory provisions of the copyright law. The licensor grants the licensee the right to sell or distribute recordings or sheet music for a fixed fee paid to the licensor or for a fee based on sales. This chapter presents the proper accounting by both the licensor and the licensee for license agreements in the recording and music industry.

The industry is currently attempting to adapt its business models for copyright protection, product distribution, and artist compensation to new electronic distribution channels. The new business models that inevitably evolve may require additional accounting guidance.

DEFINITIONS OF TERMS

License agreements. Contractual arrangements entered into by an owner (licensor) of a master or music copyright and a licensee that grant the licensee the right to sell or distribute recordings or sheet music for a fixed fee paid to the licensor or for a fee based on sales.

REVENUE RECOGNITION BY LICENSORS

A license agreement is considered an outright sale when the licensor has

1. Signed a noncancelable contract.
2. Agreed to accept a specified fee.
3. Transferred the music rights to the licensee, who is able to use them.
4. Fulfilled all significant duties owed the licensee.

When all of these conditions are met, the earnings process is complete and revenue is recognized if there is reasonable assurance that the license fee is fully collectible.

In some cases the licensee pays a minimum guarantee, which is an amount paid in advance to a licensor for the right to sell or distribute recordings or sheet music. A minimum guarantee is first recorded by the licensor as a liability and then amortized to income as the license fee is earned. If the amount of the fee that is earned is indeterminable, then straight-line recognition of revenue from the guarantee is required over the license period.

Example

A licensor receives a $10,000 minimum guarantee under a five-year license agreement. The entry to record the receipt of cash is

Cash	10,000	
Liability under license agreement		10,000

The licensor recognizes revenue from the guarantee on a straight-line basis. At the end of each year of the license period, the licensor records the following entry:

Liability under license agreement	2,000	
License fees earned (revenue)		2,000

A licensor may charge fees for such items as free recordings beyond a certain number given away by a recording club. The amount of such fees is not determinable when the license agreement is made. Therefore, the licensor can recognize revenue only when the amount can be reasonably estimated or when the license agreement expires.

12 REVENUE RECOGNITION FOR SERVICES

OVERVIEW

Services represent over half of the transactions completed in the U.S. economy, but there are no official pronouncements that provide specific accounting standards for them. Accounting for service transactions has evolved primarily through industry practice, and as a result, different accounting methods have developed to apply the fundamental principles of revenue and cost recognition. In fact, different accounting methods are used by similar entities for practically identical transactions.

DEFINITIONS OF TERMS

Collection method. A method that recognizes revenue when cash is collected.

Completed performance method. A method that recognizes revenue after the last significant act has been completed.

Direct costs. Costs that are related specifically to the performance of services under a contract or other arrangement.

Indirect costs. Costs that are incurred as a result of service activities that are not directly allocable to specific contracts or customer arrangements.

Initiation fee. A onetime, up-front charge that gives the purchaser the privilege of using a service or facilities.

Installation fee. A one-time, up-front charge for making equipment operational so that it functions as intended.

Out-of-pocket costs. Costs incurred incidental to the performance of services that are often reimbursable to the service firm by the customer either at actual cost or at an agreed-upon rate (e.g., meals, lodging, airfare, taxi fares, etc.).

Precontract or preengagement costs. Costs incurred prior to execution of a service contract or engagement letter.

Product transaction. A transaction between a seller and a purchaser in which the seller supplies tangible merchandise to the purchaser.

Proportional performance method. A method that recognizes revenue on the basis of the number of acts performed in relation to the total number of acts to be performed.

Service transaction. A transaction between a seller and a purchaser in which the seller performs work, or agrees to maintain a readiness to perform work, for the purchaser.

Specific performance method. A method that recognizes revenue after one specific act has been performed.

SERVICE TRANSACTIONS

The American Institute of Certified Public Accountants (AICPA) has defined service transactions as follows:

> ...*transactions between a seller and a purchaser in which, for a mutually agreed price, the seller performs, agrees to perform, agrees to perform at a later date, or agrees to maintain readiness to perform an act or acts, including permitting others to use enterprise resources that do not alone produce a tangible commodity or product as the principal intended result.*

GAAP requires that revenue generally be recognized when (1) it is realized or realizable and (2) it has been earned. With respect to service transactions, the AICPA concluded

> ...*revenue from service transactions [is to] be based on performance, because performance determines the extent to which the earnings process is complete or virtually complete.*

In practice, performance may involve the execution of a defined act, a set of similar or identical acts, or a set of related but not similar or identical acts. Performance may also occur with the passage of time. Accordingly, one of the following four methods (which will be described later in the "Revenue Recognition Methods" section) can serve as a guideline for the recognition of revenue from service transactions:

1. The specific performance method
2. The proportional performance method
3. The completed performance method
4. The collection method

SERVICE VS. PRODUCT TRANSACTIONS

Many transactions involve the sale of a tangible product and a service; therefore, for proper accounting treatment, it must be determined whether the transaction is primarily a service transaction accompanied by an incidental product, primarily a product transaction accompanied by an incidental service, or a sale in which both a service transaction and a product transaction occur. The following criteria apply:

1. **Service transactions.** If the seller offers both a service and a product in a single transaction and if the terms of the agreement for the sale of the service are worded in such a manner that the inclusion or exclusion of the product would not change the total transaction price, the product is incidental to the rendering of the service; the transaction is a service transaction that is accounted for in accordance with one of the four methods presented. For example, fixed-price equipment maintenance contracts that include parts at no additional charge are service transactions.

2. **Product transactions.** If the seller offers both a service and a product in a single transaction and if the terms of the agreement for the sale of the product are worded in such a manner that the inclusion or exclusion of the service would not change the total transaction price, the rendering of the service is incidental to the sale of the product; the transaction is a product transaction that is accounted for as such. For example, the sale of a product accompanied by a guarantee or warranty for repair is considered a product transaction.

3. **Service and product transactions.** If the seller offers both a product and a service and the agreement states the product and service are separate elements such that the inclusion or exclusion of the service would vary the total transaction price, the transaction consists of two components: a product transaction that is accounted for separately as such, and a service transaction that is accounted for in accordance with one of the four accepted methods.

REVENUE RECOGNITION METHODS

Once a transaction is determined to be a service transaction, one of the following four methods is used to recognize revenue. The method chosen is to be based on the nature and extent of the service(s) to be performed:

1. **Specific performance method.** The specific performance method is used when performance consists of the execution of a single act. Revenue is recognized at the time the act takes place. For example, a stockbroker records sales commissions as revenue upon the sale of a client's investment.

2. **Proportional performance method.** The proportional performance method is used when performance consists of a number of identical or similar acts.

   a. If the service transaction involves a specified number of identical or similar acts, an equal amount of revenue is recorded for each act performed. For example, a refuse disposal company recognizes an equal amount of revenue for each weekly removal of a customer's garbage.

   b. If the service transaction involves a specified number of defined but not identical or similar acts, the revenue recognized for each act is based on the following formula:

$$\frac{\text{Direct cost of individual act}}{\begin{array}{c}\text{Total estimated direct costs}\\ \text{of the transaction}\end{array}} \times \begin{array}{c}\text{Total revenues from}\\ \text{complete transaction}\end{array}$$

   For example, a correspondence school that provides lessons, examinations, and grading would use this method. If the measurements suggested in the preceding equation are impractical or not objectively determinable, revenue is recognized on a systematic and rational basis that reasonably relates revenue recognition to service performance.

   c. If the service transaction involves an unspecified number of acts over a fixed time period for performance, revenue is recognized over the period during which the acts will be performed by using the straight-line method unless a better method of relating revenue and performance is appropriate. For example, a health club might recognize revenue on a straight-line basis over the term of a member's membership. Many professional service firms record revenues on their engagements on an "as-performed basis" by valuing labor time, as expended, at a standard hourly billing rate and accumulating these amounts as an asset, work-in-progress (WIP). For periodic reporting, ending balances of WIP (and the related revenue recognized) must be adjusted by recording valuation allowances for unbillable or unrealizable WIP.

Example of proportional performance revenue recognition

The Cheyenne Snow Removal Company enters into a contract with the Western Office Tower to plow its parking lot. The contract states that Cheyenne will receive a fixed payment of $500 to clear Western's central parking lot whenever snowfall exceeds two inches. Following an unusually snowy winter, Western elects to cap its snow removal costs by tying Cheyenne into an annual $18,000 fixed price for snow removal, no matter how many snowstorms occur. Snowfall is not predictable by month, and can occur over as much as a six-month period. Western pays the full amount in advance, resulting in the following entry by Cheyenne:

Cash	18,000	
Customer advances		18,000

Though Cheyenne could recognize revenue on a straight-line basis through the contract period, it chooses to tie recognition more closely to actual performance with the proportional performance method. Its total estimated direct cost through the contract period is likely to be $12,600, based on its average costs in previous years. There is one snowstorm in October, which costs Cheyenne $350 for snow removal under the Western contract. Cheyenne's revenue recognition calculation in October is

$$\frac{\$350 \text{ direct cost}}{\$12,600 \text{ total direct cost}} \times \$18,000 \text{ total revenue} = \$500 \text{ revenue recognition}$$

Thus, Cheyenne recognizes a gross margin of $150 during the month. By the end of February, Cheyenne has conducted snow removal 28 times at the same margin, resulting in revenue recognition of $14,000 and a gross margin of $4,200. Cheyenne's cumulative entry for all performance under the Western contract to date is as follows:

Customer advances	14,000	
Direct labor expense	9,800	
Revenue		14,000
Cash		9,800

In March, Cheyenne removes snow 12 more times at a cost of $4,200. Its initial revenue recognition calculation during this month is

$$\frac{\$4,200 \text{ direct cost}}{\$12,600 \text{ total direct cost}} \times \$18,000 \text{ total revenue} = \$6,000 \text{ revenue recognition}$$

However, this would result in total revenue recognition of $20,000, which exceeds the contract fixed fee by $2,000. Accordingly, Cheyenne only recognizes sufficient revenue to maximize the contract cap, resulting in a loss of $200 for the month.

Customer advances	4,000	
Direct labor expense	4,200	
Revenue		4,000
Cash		4,200

3. **Completed performance method.** The completed performance method is used when more than one act must be performed and when the final act is so significant to the entire transaction taken as a whole that performance cannot be considered to have taken place until the performance of that final act occurs. For example, a moving company packs, loads, and transports merchandise; however, the final act of delivering the merchandise is so significant

that revenue is not recognized until the goods reach their intended destination. If the services are to be performed in an indeterminable number of acts over an indeterminable period of time and if an objective measure for estimating the degree to which performance has taken place cannot be found, revenue is recognized under the completed performance method.

4. **Collection method.** The collection method is used in circumstances when there is a significant degree of uncertainty surrounding the collection of service revenue. Under this method, revenue is not recognized until the cash is collected. For example, personal services may be provided to a customer whose ability to pay is uncertain.

Exhibit 11.1 shows the criteria under which one should use either the collection, completed performance, specific performance, or proportional performance methods. The flowchart is designed to show that, unless various revenue-related problems exist in a service contract, the proportional performance method is the default revenue recording method.

Exhibit 11.1: Decision tree for recording service revenues

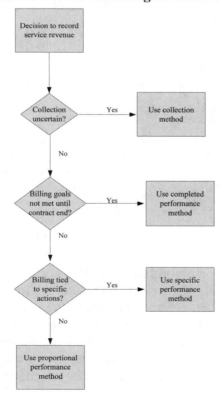

EXPENSE RECOGNITION

GAAP, in general, requires that costs be recognized as expense in the period that the revenue with which they are associated is recognized (the matching principle). Costs are deferred only when they are expected to be recoverable from future revenues. When applying these principles to service transactions, special consideration must be given to the different types of costs that might arise. The major classifications of costs arising from service transactions are as follows:

1. **Precontract or preengagement costs.** These are costs that are incurred before the service contract (or engagement letter in many professional services firms) has been executed between the parties. They can include legal fees for negotiating contract terms, costs of credit investigations, and the salaries and benefits of individuals involved in negotiating contracts with prospective clients. (See the related discussion in Chapter 7, Revenue Recognition for Long-Term Construction Contracts.)
2. **Direct costs.** Costs that are specifically attributable to providing service under a specific contract or contracts. For example, this would include service labor and repair parts on a fixed-price maintenance contract.
3. **Indirect costs.** Costs that are incurred as a result of all service activity but that are not directly allocable to any specific contracts or engagements.
4. **Out-of-pocket costs.** Costs incurred incidental to the performance of services that are often reimbursable to the service firm by the customer either at actual cost or at an agreed-upon rate (e.g., meals, lodging, airfare, taxi fare, etc.).
5. **Overhead.** General costs of running the business that do not fall into any of the above categories, often referred to as selling, general, and administrative expenses. These include uncollectible receivables, advertising, sales commissions, and facility costs (depreciation, rent, maintenance, etc.).

The costs listed above are accounted for as follows:

1. **Precontract or preengagement costs.** Expense as incurred as start-up costs for all of the service revenue recognition methods.
2. **Direct costs.** Expense as incurred under all of the service revenue recognition methods because of the close correlation between the amount of direct costs incurred and the extent of performance achieved. Direct costs incurred prior to performance, referred to as

initial direct costs (e.g., expendable materials purchased for use on the job/engagement that are purchased and held by the service enterprise as a form of inventory), are deferred and recorded as prepayments (or supplies inventory, depending on the nature of the item). Under the specific performance or completed performance methods, these costs are recognized as expenses at the time of service performance at the point that revenue is recognized. Under the proportional performance method, initial direct costs are charged to expense in proportion to the recognition of service revenue (i.e., by applying the ratio of revenues recognized in the period to total expected revenues over the life of the contract).

3. **Indirect costs.** Under all of the revenue recognition methods, indirect costs are expensed as incurred.
4. **Out-of-pocket costs.** Under all of the revenue recognition methods, out-of-pocket costs are expensed as incurred with the related client billings presented as revenue in the statement of income.
5. **Overhead.** Under all of the revenue recognition methods, overhead is expensed as incurred.

Losses on service transactions are recognized when direct costs incurred to date plus estimated remaining direct costs of performance exceed the current estimated net realizable revenue from the contract. The loss (given as the Direct costs incurred to date + Estimated remaining direct costs – Estimated realizable revenue) is first applied to reduce any recorded deferred costs to zero, with any remaining loss recognized on the income statement and credited to an estimated liability.

INITIATION AND INSTALLATION FEES

Many service transactions also involve the charging of a nonrefundable initiation or activation fee with subsequent periodic payments for future services and/or a nonrefundable fee for installation of equipment essential to providing future services with subsequent periodic payments for the services. These nonrefundable fees may, in substance, be partly or wholly advance charges for future services.

Initiation or Activation Fees

If there is an objectively determinable value for the right or privilege granted by the fee, that value is recognized as revenue on the initiation date. Any related direct costs are recognized as expense on the initiation date. If the value of the right or privilege cannot be objectively determined, the fee is recorded as a liability for future services and recognized as revenue in accordance with one of the revenue recognition methods.

Installation Fees

If the equipment and its installation costs are essential for the service to be provided and if customers cannot normally purchase the equipment in a separate transaction, the installation fee is considered an advance charge for future services. The fee is recognized as revenue over the estimated service period. The costs of installation and the installed equipment are amortized over the period the equipment is expected to generate revenue. If customers can normally purchase the equipment in a separate transaction, the installation fee is part of a product transaction that is accounted for separately as such.

Example of installation fees

Vintner Corporation has invented a nitrogen injection device for resealing opened wine bottles, calling it NitroSeal. The device is especially useful for restaurants, which can seal wine bottles opened for customers who want to take home unfinished wine. Because the NitroSeal device is massive, Vintner pays a third party to install each unit for a fixed fee of $200, charging restaurants a $300 nonrefundable installation fee plus a monthly fee for a 20-month cancelable contract. The initial entries to record an installation charge from a supplier and related installation billing to a customer are as follows:

Installation asset	200	
Accounts payable		200
Accounts receivable	300	
Unearned installation fees (liability)		300

Vintner recognizes the installation revenue and associated installation expense for each installation in 1/20 increments to match the contract length, each with the following entry:

Unearned installation fees	15	
Installation revenue		15
Installation expense	10	
Installation asset		10

A customer cancels its contract with Vintner after five months. As a result, Vintner accelerates all remaining amortization on the installation asset and recognizes all remaining unearned installation fees at once, using the following entries:

Unearned installation fees	225	
Installation revenue		225
Installation expense	150	
Installation asset		150

If the service contract had included a clause for a refundable installation fee, then cancellation after five months would still have resulted in immediate acceleration of amortization on the installation asset. However, the unearned installation revenue could not be recognized. Instead, the following entry would have recorded the return of the installation fee:

Unearned installation fees	225	
Cash		225

OTHER GUIDANCE TO ACCOUNTING FOR SERVICE TRANSACTIONS

Several miscellaneous topics related to service transactions are discussed in the following paragraphs.

Reporting Reimbursable Costs

While not limited to service providers, a common situation for many professional service providers is the incurrence of costs that are later billed to clients, with or without a markup over actual cost. Examples of out-of-pocket expenses include meals, lodging, airfare, taxi fares, and so on. Prior practice had been varied, with many reporting entities showing reimbursements, implicitly as offsets to expenses; others reported such reimbursements as revenue. While the net effect on reported earnings was the same under either approach, certain key performance measures, such as gross revenue, could vary considerably depending on choice of accounting method. Any billings for out-of-pocket costs are to be classified as revenue in the statement of income and not as a reduction in expenses. This guidance is equally applicable whether expenses are billed to clients (1) as a pass-through, (i.e., at actual cost to the service firm without a markup), (2) at a marked-up amount, or (3) are included in the billing rate or negotiated price for the services.

Separately Priced Extended Warranties

Extended warranties provide additional protection beyond that of the manufacturer's original warranty, lengthen the period of coverage specified in the manufacturer's original warranty, or both. Similarly, a product maintenance contract is an agreement for services to maintain a product for a certain length of time. Clearly, revenue recognition at inception is not acceptable, and it is often impossible to estimate the actual pattern of service that will be provided to the customers over the terms of the contracts. Revenue from these contracts should be deferred and recognized on a straight-line basis unless evidence exists that costs are incurred on some other basis. If so, revenue is allocated to each period using the ratio of the period's cost to estimated total cost.

Direct costs of obtaining extended warranty or maintenance contracts are to be capitalized and recognized as expense in the ratio that revenues recognized each period bear to total anticipated revenues from the respective contracts. Any other costs are charged to expense as incurred. Losses on these contracts are recognized immediately if the sum of the future costs and remaining unamortized direct acquisition costs exceed the related unearned revenue. When recognizing a loss, any unamortized acquisition costs are first charged to expense, and a liability for any remaining loss is then recorded.

Example of a separately priced product maintenance contract

Salomon Heating enters into a four-year product maintenance contract with Everly Manufacturing, under which Salomon will conduct preventive maintenance and repairs to Everly's heating systems. Under the contract terms, Salomon bills Everly $1,000 during each month of the contract period, and recognizes the billed amount as revenue at once. This equates to straight-line recognition of the total contract amount.

Salomon incurred a $4,000 legal expense in writing the contract with Everly, as well as a $1,600 commission, both of which it defers and amortizes over the contract period. During the first month of work, Salomon incurs direct costs of $650 in wages, as well as $200 of repair-related materials. Its charge to expense entry follows:

Cost of goods sold—materials	200	
Cost of goods sold—labor	650	
Legal expense	83	
Commission expense	33	
Inventory—spare parts		200
Cash		650
Deferred legal costs		83
Deferred commission costs		33

At the end of two years, Salomon realizes that it must rebuild Everly's boiler. The rebuild will cost $10,000, while all expected future maintenance work will cost an additional $20,000. Unamortized legal costs equal $2,000 and unamortized commissions equal $800, while unearned revenue is $24,000. Salomon must recognize a loss of $8,800, which is the difference between all expected costs of $32,800 and unearned revenue of $24,000. To do so, Salomon accelerates all remaining amortization of the capitalized legal and commission assets, and recognizes a liability for the remainder of the loss with the following entry:

Commission expense	800	
Legal expense	2,000	
Loss on contractual obligation	6,000	
Deferred commission costs		800
Deferred legal costs		2,000
Unfulfilled contractual obligations (liability)		6,000

Salomon rebuilds Everly's boiler at the expected cost of $10,000. Since this is one-third of the remaining costs to be incurred under the contract, Salomon recognizes one-third of the $6,000 unfulfilled contractual obligation that was used to offset the loss, and charges the rest of the cost to expense with the following entry:

Unfulfilled contractual obligations (liability)	2,000	
Cost of goods sold—labor	8,000	
Cash		10,000

SERVICE REVENUE DISCLOSURES

A membership organization should describe the types of membership fees charged and the method used to recognize revenue. The footnote can also reveal the amount of unrecognized revenue currently listed as a liability. Two examples are as follows:

1. The club charges a onetime nonrefundable membership fee of $10,000, as well as monthly dues of $300. Since members have no right to the return of the initial fee, the club recognizes this amount in its entirety when paid. Monthly dues are recognized when billed. There is no liability associated with unrecognized revenue shown on the balance sheet.
2. The club charges a onetime membership fee of $10,000, which can be repaid to members if they choose to resign from the club, less a $500 termination fee. The club holds all membership fees in escrow and only recognizes the termination fee when members resign from the club. The total amount of membership fees currently held in escrow is $1,620,000, and is listed under the Membership Fees Held in Reserve liability account. The club also charges $300 monthly dues, which are recognized when billed.

As is the case with any long-term service revenue contract, the period over which warranty revenues are calculated should be described, if this is a significant proportion of revenues. For many companies, this is a small revenue component not requiring separate disclosure. If it is disclosed, note the term over which warranty revenues are recognized and the amount of unrecognized warranty revenues. A sample footnote is as follows:

The company sells a one-year warranty agreement with its kitchen appliances; warranty revenues comprise approximately 8% of total revenues. These revenues are recognized ratably over their service periods, with the unrecognized balance listed as a short-term liability in the Unrecognized Warranty Revenues account. The unrecognized balance of these sales was $850,000 as of the balance sheet date.

SERVICE REVENUE POLICIES AND PROCEDURES

If service revenue is recognized under the specific performance method, then the billing procedure should include a policy that invoices are not to be created prior to the completion of all service work, evidence of which must be a service completion certificate that is signed and dated by the customer.

If a service contract requires work to be performed over a considerable period of time, it is customary for the company to create a job in its time-keeping system, against which employees record their hours worked. However, once the job is completed, there is a risk that the job number will remain open, with additional hours continuing to mistakenly be charged against it. To avoid this problem, the month-end closing procedure should include a requirement to review all open job numbers and close those for which all service work and related billings have been completed.

A company is unlikely to record losses on service transactions prior to the completion of a service contract, because this action falls outside the normal billing process. Accordingly, the month-end closing procedure should include a requirement that all service contracts still open after month-end billings be examined for potential losses, which are to be recorded at once.

The following procedure can be used to periodically review service contracts to determine the existence of any projected contract losses:

1. Summarize all project-to-date direct costs from the relevant general ledger account.
2. Go to the project manager and review the amount of estimated costs yet to be incurred on the project. Compare this amount to the estimated completion cost from the last review to see if there are any unusual changes, and discuss the differences. Also verify the cost estimated against any project planning database, such as a Gantt or Critical Path Method chart.
3. Summarize all project billings to date, and verify the amount of remaining billings, adjusted for any contract modifications.

4. Combine the actual and estimated costs and subtract them from the total expected project revenues. If the costs exceed revenues, notify the controller of the difference with a memo, outlining the reasons for the loss.

5. Debit the Loss on Contracts account for the amount of the estimated loss. Use the offsetting credit to eliminate any unrecognized costs stored in an asset account, and credit the remaining loss to the Estimated Loss on Service Contracts account.

SERVICE REVENUE CONTROLS

If a company recognizes revenue under the specific performance method, then the key determinant of revenue recognition is the date of service completion. Accordingly, an internal audit program should require a periodic comparison of the invoice date and the documented date of service completion, to ensure that revenue recognition did not occur prior to service completion. A more difficult analysis would be to review customer service logs to determine if customer complaints were received subsequent to the alleged service completion date, indicating that service was not actually completed on the documented date.

The proportional performance method is the most aggressive service revenue calculation method, in that revenues can be recognized earlier than with most other revenue recognition methods. For this control, trace each revenue-creation journal entry back to the related service contract and verify that collection is reasonably assured and that billings are not tied to specific actions. If either of these cases hold true, other more conservative revenue recognition methods must be used that may reduce the amount of revenue recognized.

Losses on service contracts must be recognized as expenses immediately, even if the losses are only estimated. Since there is a natural reluctance to recognize losses in advance of the actual event, a good control is to include a standard review of estimated losses on service contracts as part of the monthly closing process.

If services are provided under the completed performance method, it is possible that the duration of the contract period is so long that the paperwork related to the service is misplaced, and no revenue recognition occurs at all. To guard against this problem, a standard billing control should be to compare the records of employee time charged against customers with the file of open sales orders, to determine if any time is being recorded against an apparently nonexistent job.

If revenue is recognized under the collection method, there should be no revenue recognition prior to the cash receipt date. To ensure that this is the case, an audit program could include a comparison of revenue recognition dates to cash receipt dates. A simplified version of this control is to match the total amount of revenue recorded to the total amount of all cash received from customers during the period—they should be identical.

A company may alter the definition of direct and other expenses, in order to shift expenses into or out of the direct cost category, which can then be shifted among different reporting periods in order to alter the reported revenue level. To verify the appropriateness of these changes, an audit program can include a review of the types of expenses being deferred as part of the revenue recognition process. At a more simplified level, this control can involve the calculation of a long-term gross margin trend line for service projects; sudden variations in the margin may indicate the shifting of expenses into or out of the direct cost category.

13 REVENUE RECOGNITION FOR SOFTWARE

OVERVIEW

Complicated issues of revenue recognition arise for enterprises that sell computer software and associated goods and services (program upgrades, maintenance agreements, etc.). This involves the recognition of revenue on software sales including multiple-element arrangements that can include the cost of the software bundled with elements of training, upgrades, and postcontract customer support (PCS).

DEFINITIONS OF TERMS

Customer support. Services performed by an enterprise to assist customers in their use of software products. Those services include any installation assistance, training classes, telephone question-and-answer services, newsletters, on-site visits, and software or data modifications.

Maintenance. Activities undertaken after the product is available for general release to customers to correct errors (commonly referred to as "bugs") or keep the product updated with current information. Those activities include routine changes and additions.

SOFTWARE REVENUE RECOGNITION

The primary revenue recognition rules for software are set forth in the following paragraphs.

Product May Not Equate with Delivery of Software

Arrangements to deliver software, whether alone or in conjunction with other products, often include services. Services to be provided in such contexts commonly involve significant production, modification, or customization of the software. Thus, physical delivery of the software might not constitute the delivery of the final product contracted for, absent those alterations, resulting in the requirement that such arrangements be accounted for as construction-type or production-type contracts. However, if the services do not entail significant production, modification, or customization of the software, the services are accounted for as a separate element.

Delivery Is the Key Threshold Issue for Revenue Recognition

This is consistent with the principles set forth in CON 5, *Recognition and Measurement in Financial Statements of Business Enterprises*, which states that

> *An entity's revenue-earning activities involve delivering or producing goods, rendering services, or other activities that constitute its ongoing major or central operations, and revenues are considered to have been earned when the entity has substantially accomplished what it must do to be entitled to the benefits represented by the revenues . . . [t]he two conditions (being realized or realizable and being earned) are usually met by the time the product or merchandise is delivered . . . to customers, and revenues . . . are commonly recognized at time of sale (usually meaning delivery).*

Revenue must be allocated to all elements of the sales arrangement, with recognition dependent upon meeting the criteria on an element-by-element basis. All obligations are accounted for and revenue is allocated to each element of the sales arrangement, based on vendor-specific objective evidence (VSOE) of the fair values of the elements.

Fair values for revenue allocation purposes must be vendor specific. When there are multiple elements of an arrangement, revenue is generally recognized on an element-by-element basis as individual elements are delivered. Revenue is allocated to the various elements in proportion to their relative fair values. This allocation process requires that VSOE of fair value be employed, regardless of any separate prices stated in the contract for each element, since prices stated in a contract may not represent fair value and, accordingly, might result in an unreasonable allocation of revenue. This approach is consistent with the accounting for commingled revenue as set forth in the current standard on accounting for franchise fee revenue. The use of surrogate prices, such as those published by competitors or industry averages, cannot be used because of the wide differences in products and services offered by vendors. Separate transaction prices for the individual elements comprising the arrangement, if they are also being sold on that basis, are the best such evidence, although under some circumstances (such as when prices in the arrangement are based on multiple users rather than the single-user pricing of the element on a stand-alone basis) even that information could conceivably be invalid for revenue allocation purposes. Relative sales prices of the elements included in the arrangement are to be used whenever possible.

The earnings process is not complete if fees are subject to forfeiture. Even when elements have been delivered, if fees allocated to those elements are subject to forfeiture, refund, or other concession if the vendor does not fulfill its delivery responsibilities relative to other elements of the arrangement, those fees are not treated as having been earned. The potential concessions are an indication that the customer would not have licensed the delivered elements without also licensing the undelivered elements. For that reason, there must be persuasive evidence that fees allocated to delivered elements are not subject to forfeiture, refund, or other concessions before revenue recognition can be justified. Thus, for example, in determining the persuasiveness of the evidence, the vendor's history of making concessions that were not required by the provisions of an arrangement is more persuasive than are terms included in the arrangement that indicate that no concessions are required.

Operational Rules

1. If an arrangement to deliver software or a software system, either alone or together with other products or services, requires significant production, modification, or customization of software, the entire arrangement is accounted for as a long-term construction contract.

2. If the arrangement does not require significant production, modification, or customization of software, revenue is recognized when all of the following criteria are met:

   a. Persuasive evidence of an arrangement exists.
   b. Delivery has occurred.
   c. The vendor's fee is fixed or determinable.
   d. Collectibility is probable.

3. For software arrangements that provide licenses for multiple software deliverables (multiple elements), some of which may be deliverable only on a when-and-if-available basis, these deliverables are considered in determining whether an arrangement includes multiple elements. The requirements with respect to arrangements that consist of multiple elements are applied to all additional products and services specified in the arrangement, including those described as being deliverable only on a when-and-if-available basis.

4. For arrangements having multiple elements, the fee is allocated to the various elements based on VSOE of fair value, regardless of any separate prices stated for each element within the contract. VSOE of fair value is limited to the following:

a. The price charged when the same element is sold separately, or

b. For an element not yet being sold separately, the price established by management, if it is probable that the price, once established, will not change before the separate introduction of the element into the marketplace.

The revenue allocated to undelivered elements cannot later be adjusted. However, if it becomes probable that the amount allocated to an undelivered element of the arrangement will result in a loss on that element, the loss must be immediately recognized. When a vendor's pricing is based on multiple factors such as the number of products and the number of users, the amount allocated to the same elements when sold separately must consider all the relevant factors of the vendor's pricing structure.

In some cases, multiple-element arrangements are not accounted for as long-term construction contracts when (1) there is VSOE of the fair values of all undelivered elements, (2) VSOE does not exist for one or more of the delivered elements, and (3) all other revenue recognition criteria have been satisfied. In such cases, the "residual" method of allocation of selling price is to be utilized. This results in deferral of the aggregate fair value of the undelivered elements of the arrangement (to be recognized later as delivery occurs), with the excess of the total arrangement fee over the deferred portion being recognized in connection with the delivered components. This change was made to accommodate the situation whereby software is commonly sold with one "free" year of support, where additional years of support are also marketed at fixed prices; in this case, the fair value of the "free" support is deferred (and amortized over the year), while the software itself is assigned a revenue amount which is the difference between the package price and the known price of one year's support.

5. If a discount is offered in a multiple-element arrangement, a proportionate amount of the discount is applied to each element included in the arrangement, based on each element's fair value without regard to the discount. However, no portion of the discount is allocated to any upgrade rights.

6. If sufficient VSOE does not exist for the allocation of revenue to the various elements of the arrangement, all revenue from the arrangement is deferred until the earlier of the point at which (1) such sufficient VSOE does exist, or (2) all elements of the arrangement have been delivered. The exceptions to this guidance are

a. If the only undelivered element is PCS, the entire fee is recognized ratably over the contractual PCS period, or when the PCS rights are implicit in the arrangement, over the period that PCS is expected to be provided to the customer.

b. If the only undelivered element is services that do not involve significant production, modification, or customization of the software (e.g., training or installation), the entire fee is recognized over the period during which the services are expected to be performed.

c. If the arrangement is in substance a subscription, the entire fee is recognized ratably over the term of the arrangement, if stated, otherwise over the estimated economic life of the products included in the arrangement.

d. If the fee is based on the number of copies delivered, how the arrangement is accounted for depends on whether the total fee is fixed, and on whether the buyer can alter the composition of the copies to be received, as follows:

(1) If the arrangement provides customers with the right to reproduce or obtain copies of two or more software products at a specified price per copy (not per product) up to the total amount of the fixed fee, an allocation of the fee to the individual products generally cannot be made, because the total revenue allocable to each software product is unknown at inception and depends on subsequent choices to be made by the customer and, sometimes, on future vendor development activity. Nevertheless, certain arrangements that include products that are not deliverable at inception impose a maximum number of copies of the undeliverable product(s) to which the customer is entitled. In such arrangements, a portion of the arrangement fee is allocated to the undeliverable product(s). This allocation is made assuming that the customer will elect to receive the maximum number of copies of the undeliverable product(s).

(2) In arrangements in which no allocation can be made until the first copy or product master of each product covered by the arrangement has been delivered to the customer, and assuming the four conditions set forth above are met, revenue is recognized as copies of delivered products are either (a) reproduced by the customer, or (b) furnished to the customer if the vendor is duplicating the software.

Once the vendor has delivered the product master or the first copy of all products covered by the arrangement, any previously unrecognized licensing fees are recognized, since only duplication of the software is required to satisfy the vendor's delivery requirement and such duplication is incidental to the arrangement. Consequently, the delivery criterion is deemed to have been met upon delivery to the customer of the product master or first copy. When the arrangement terminates, the vendor recognizes any licensing fees not previously recognized. Revenue is not recognized fully until at least one of the following conditions is met: either (a) delivery is complete for all products covered by the arrangement, or (b) the aggregate revenue attributable to all copies of the software products delivered is equal to the fixed fee, provided that the vendor is not obligated to deliver additional software products under the arrangement.

(3)   The revenue allocated to the delivered products is recognized when the product master or first copy is delivered. If, during the term of the arrangement, the customer reproduces or receives enough copies of these delivered products so that revenue allocable to the delivered products exceeds the revenue previously recognized, the additional revenue is recognized as the copies are reproduced or delivered. The revenue allocated to the undeliverable product(s) is reduced by a corresponding amount.

7. The portion of the fee allocated to a contract element is recognized when the four revenue recognition criteria are met with respect to the element. In applying those criteria, the delivery of an element is considered not to have occurred if there are undelivered elements that are essential to the functionality of the delivered element, because functionality of the delivered element is considered to be impaired.

8. No portion of the fee can be deemed to be collectible if the portion of the fee allocable to delivered elements is subject to forfeiture, refund, or other concession if any of the undelivered elements are not delivered. If management represents that it will not provide refunds or concessions that are not required under the provisions of the arrangement, this assertion must be supported by reference to all available evidence. This evidence may include the following:

a. Acknowledgment in the arrangement regarding products not currently available or not to be delivered currently
b. Separate prices stipulated in the arrangement for each deliverable element
c. Default and damage provisions as defined in the arrangement
d. Enforceable payment obligations and due dates for the delivered elements that are not dependent on the delivery of future deliverable elements, coupled with the intent of the vendor to enforce rights of payment
e. Installation and use of the delivered software
f. Support services, such as telephone support, related to the delivered software being provided currently by the vendor

OTHER ACCOUNTING GUIDANCE

Disclosure of Software Revenue Recognition

When a company sells computer software, it should disclose its revenue recognition policy for separating the various elements of a software sale and recognizing each portion of it. An example follows:

> Approximately 80% of the Company's sales are from computer software and related maintenance agreements. The company splits these sales into their software and maintenance components and recognizes the software portion of the sales at once. The maintenance portion of the sales is initially recorded in an Unrecognized Maintenance Service Agreements liability account and recognized ratably over the term of the agreements, which are either 3 or 12 months. In cases where the software and maintenance components of a sale are not clearly differentiated in a sale contract, the Company estimates the relative price of each component based on its separate retail price. As of the balance sheet date, there was approximately $725,000 of unrecognized maintenance sales in the Unrecognized Maintenance Service Agreements account.
>
> In software arrangements that include rights to multiple software products, specified upgrades, maintenance or services, the Company allocates the total arrangement fee among each deliverable using the fair value of each of the deliverables determined using vendor-specific objective evidence. Vendor-specific objective evidence of fair value is determined using the price charged when that element is sold separately. In software arrangements in which the Company has fair value of all undelivered elements but not of a delivered element, the residual method is used to record revenue. Under the residual method, the fair value of the undelivered elements is deferred and the remaining portion of the arrangement fee is allocated to the delivered element(s) and is recognized as revenue. In software arrangements in which the Company does not have vendor-specific objective evidence of fair value

of all undelivered elements, revenue is deferred until fair value is determined or all elements for which the Company does not have vendor-specific objective evidence of fair value have been delivered.

14 OTHER REVENUE RECOGNITION ACCOUNTING TOPICS

OVERVIEW

The major categories of revenue-generating transactions, for which specialized accounting standards have been developed, have been addressed in the earlier chapters of this book. In the following sections, various miscellaneous revenue-related requirements are discussed.

RECOGNITION OF FEES FOR GUARANTEEING A LOAN

When an entity guarantees repayment of a borrower's obligation and charges the borrower a fee for this service, the guarantor should recognize fee income over the guarantee period, and disclose the guarantee if it is material. The guarantor should also periodically assess the probability of loss to determine if a liability or loss should be recognized.

SALES OF FUTURE REVENUES

A company may receive cash from an investor in return for an agreement to pay that investor a predetermined percentage or amount of future revenue or income. In determining whether the company should record the proceeds from the investor as debt or deferred income, the presence of any of the following factors creates a rebuttable presumption that the proceeds should be classified as debt:

1. The form of the transaction is debt.
2. The company is actively involved in the generation of cash flows to be paid to the investor.
3. The transaction is cancelable by payment of a lump sum or assets.
4. The investor's rate of return is limited by the terms of the transaction.
5. Variations in the company's revenue or income have only a minor impact on the investor's rate of return.
6. The investor has some kind of recourse to the company relating to payments due.

REVENUE RECOGNITION ON SALES WITH A GUARANTEED MINIMUM RESALE VALUE

A manufacturer may sell equipment using a sales incentive clause guaranteeing that customers will receive a minimum resale amount at the time of equipment disposition. This minimum resale value guarantee may involve either the reacquisition of the equipment at a guaranteed price, or payment of the customer for any deficiency. Under this scenario, the manufacturer cannot record the transaction as a sale, but rather as a lease. As a lease, the net proceeds from the initial transaction should be recorded as a liability by the manufacturer, which is then recognized into income on a pro rata basis over the life of the lease. When the customer sells the equipment, the liability should be reduced by any amount paid to the customer as part of the guarantee. Any remaining balance in the liability account should then be recognized as income.

REVENUE RECOGNITION ON EQUIPMENT SOLD AND SUBSEQUENTLY REPURCHASED SUBJECT TO AN OPERATING LEASE

A manufacturer may sell its goods to a dealer, who then sells the goods to a customer, who may finance the purchase through a lease arrangement provided by the manufacturer or an affiliate of the manufacturer. The manufacturer can recognize revenue on the initial sale of its goods to the dealer, despite its subsequent involvement in the leasing arrangement, if all of the following conditions exist:

1. The dealer is a substantive and independent enterprise.
2. The dealer has taken ownership of the goods, which have been delivered to the dealer.
3. The manufacturer's finance affiliate has no obligation to provide a lease to the customer.
4. The customer can select from a variety of financing alternatives, which include parties unaffiliated with the manufacturer.

ACCOUNTING FOR ADVERTISING BARTER TRANSACTIONS

Some organizations exchange rights to advertise on each other's behalf, and record an equal amount of revenue for the advertising they "sell," and expense for the advertising they buy from the other entity. This should only occur if the fair value of the advertising sold can be determined through actual sale transactions within the preceding six months with unrelated parties who pay cash for this service. If the fair value cannot be determined, then no revenue can be recognized. Fair value cannot be determined based on sale transactions occurring after the barter transaction. Further, the advertising transactions being used in the fair value comparison, and for which cash was paid, must be similar to the advertising being surrendered in the barter transaction with respect to the following items:

1. Circulation, exposure, or saturation within an intended market
2. Timing
3. Prominence of display, in terms of size and location
4. Demographics of readers, viewers, or customers
5. Advertising duration

A past advertising transaction settled in cash can serve as evidence only for the fair value of an equivalent dollar amount of advertising surrendered in a barter transaction, after which it cannot be used again as evidence for the fair value determination of any other barter transaction.

Disclosure should include the amount of revenue and expense recognized from barter transactions. If the fair value of such transactions cannot be determined, then disclosure should instead include the volume and type of advertising surrendered and received.

ACCOUNTING BY A GRANTEE FOR AN EQUITY INSTRUMENT TO BE RECEIVED IN CONJUNCTION WITH PROVIDING GOODS OR SERVICES

In exchange for goods or services, an entity (the grantee) may receive equity instruments that have conversion or exercisability terms that vary based on future events, such as the attainment of sales levels or a successful initial public offering.

The grantee measures the fair value of the equity instruments received using the stock price and measurement assumptions as of the earlier of two dates. The first is the date on which the grantee and the issuer reach a mutual understanding of both the terms of the equity-based compensation and the goods to be delivered (or services to be performed). The second date is the date at which the performance necessary to earn the equity is completed by the grantee, that is, the grantee's rights have vested.

If the terms of the equity agreement are dependent on the achievement of a market condition, the fair value of the instrument is to include the effects on fair value of the commitment to change the terms if the market condition is met. Pricing models are available to value path-dependent equity instruments.

If the terms of the equity agreement are dependent on the achievement of certain performance goals (beyond those that initially established the goods to be delivered or services to be performed), the fair value of the instrument is computed without the effects of the commitment to change the terms if the goals are met. If those goals are subsequently met, the fair value is adjusted to reflect the new terms and the adjustment is reported as additional revenue.

ACCOUNTING FOR SHIPPING AND HANDLING FEES AND COSTS

All shipping and handling billings to a customer in a sale transaction must be classified as revenue.

ACCOUNTING FOR "POINTS" AND CERTAIN OTHER TIME-BASED OR VOLUME-BASED SALES INCENTIVE OFFERS, AND OFFERS FOR FREE PRODUCTS OR SERVICES TO BE DELIVERED IN THE FUTURE

Offers for cash rebates or refunds should be classified as a reduction of revenue. This reduction should be based on a systematic and rational allocation of the cost of honoring rebates or refunds earned and claimed to each of the underlying revenue transactions that result in progress by the customer toward earning the rebate or refund. If the amount of future cash rebates and refunds can be reasonably estimated, then this amount shall be based on the estimated number of customers that will eventually earn and claim rebates or refunds under the offer. Alternatively, if this amount cannot be reasonably estimated (which may be caused by an excessively long rebate or refund period, no historical experience, or the absence of a large volume of homogeneous transactions), then a liability must be established for the maximum potential refund or rebate.

The amount of a cash rebate or refund may be based on the size of a customer's purchase transaction (e.g., a 10% rebate if 500 units are ordered, or a 15% rebate if 1,000 units are ordered). If the volume of a customer's future purchases that will lead to a revision in the amount of the cash rebate or refund cannot be reasonably estimated, then the maximum cash rebate or refund factor (such as the 15% value used in the example) should be used to record a liability.

Changes in the estimated amount of cash rebates or refunds require an immediate adjustment of the balance of the rebate obligation to match the revised estimate.

ACCOUNTING IN A BUSINESS COMBINATION FOR DEFERRED REVENUE OF AN ACQUIREE

An acquiring entity may purchase an acquiree that may have recorded a liability for deferred revenue. If so, the acquiring entity should recognize a liability for this deferred revenue if it is acquiring a legal performance obligation. A legal performance obligation could be construed as the provision of goods or services, or other consideration given to a customer. The amount assigned to that liability should be based on its fair value at the date of acquisition.

ACCOUNTING FOR CONSIDERATION GIVEN BY A VENDOR TO A CUSTOMER

There is specific accounting for the consideration given by a vendor to purchasers of the vendor's products. This consideration can be provided to a purchaser at any point along the distribution chain, irrespective of whether the purchaser receiving the consideration is a direct or indirect customer of the vendor. Examples of arrangements include, but are not limited to, sales incentive offers labeled as discounts, coupons, rebates, and "free" products or services as well as arrangements referred to as slotting fees, cooperative advertising, and buy-downs.

The key issues are

1. Cash consideration given by a vendor to a customer is presumed to be a reduction of selling price and is classified as a reduction of revenue when recognized in the vendor's income statement. That presumption is overcome and the consideration is classified as a cost incurred if, and to the extent that, both of the following conditions are met:

    a. The vendor receives, or will receive, an identifiable benefit (goods or services) in exchange for the consideration. In order to meet this condition, the identified benefit must be of a type that the vendor could have acquired in an exchange transaction with a party other than a purchaser of its products or services; that is, that the benefit must be separable from the sale of the vendor's goods or services.

    b. The vendor can reasonably estimate the fair value of that identifiable benefit. If the amount of consideration paid by the vendor exceeds the estimated fair value of the benefit received, that excess amount is classified as a reduction of revenue when recognized in the vendor's income statement.

If the consideration is a "free" product or service or anything other than cash (including "credits" that the customer can apply against trade amounts owed to the vendor) or equity instruments, the cost of the consideration is characterized as an expense (as opposed to a reduction of revenue) when recognized in the vendor's income statement.

2. The amounts representing reduced revenue are classified as expense only if a vendor can demonstrate that classification of those amounts as a reduction of revenue results in negative revenue for a specific customer on a cumulative basis (that is, since the inception of the overall relationship between the vendor and the customer). However, classification as an expense would not be appropriate if a supply arrangement exists that either

   a. Provides the vendor with the right to be a provider of a certain type or class of goods or services for a specified period of time and it is probable that the customer will order the vendor's goods or services, or

   b. Requires the customer to order a minimum amount of goods or services from the vendor in the future, except to the extent that the consideration given exceeds future revenue from the customer under the arrangement.

3. If the consideration (in the form of products, services, or cash) offered voluntarily by a vendor and without charge to customers can be used or becomes exercisable by a customer as a result of a single exchange transaction, and that consideration will not result in a loss on the sale, the vendor recognizes the "cost" of the consideration at the later of the following:

   a. The date the related revenue is recognized by the vendor, or

   b. The date the sales incentive is offered. (For example, a vendor recognizes a liability for a mail-in rebate coupon that requires proof of purchase, based on the estimated amount of refunds or rebates that will be claimed by customers.)

4. If the consideration (in the form of products, services, or cash) offered voluntarily by a vendor and without charge to customers can be used or becomes exercisable by a customer as a result of a single exchange transaction, and that consideration results in a loss on the sale, a vendor does not recognize a liability prior to the date on which the related revenue is recognized (this would be improper matching). However, the offer of consideration in an amount that will result in a loss on the sale of a product may indicate an impairment of existing inventory.

5. If a vendor offers a customer a rebate or refund of a specified amount of cash consideration that is redeemable only if the customer completes a specified cumulative level of purchases or remains a customer for a specified time, the vendor recognizes the cost of the offer in a systematic and rational manner over the period in which the underlying revenue transactions that qualify the customer for the rebate or refund take place. Measurement of the total rebate or refund obligation is based on the estimated number of customers that will ultimately earn and claim rebates or refunds under the offer. If the amount cannot be reasonably estimated, the maximum potential amount is to be recognized.

ACCOUNTING BY A CUSTOMER FOR CERTAIN CONSIDERATION RECEIVED FROM A VENDOR

In general, cash consideration received from a vendor is a purchase-price concession that should be recognized by the customer as a reduction of cost of goods sold (and/or the inventory of unsold units). This presumption is overcome if payment of the consideration is for either

1. **Delivery of goods and/or services.** Payment to the customer in exchange for goods or services delivered to the vendor is accounted for by the customer as revenue. In order for the customer to recognize revenue, the goods and/or services must be "sufficiently separable" from the customer's purchase of the vendor's products by meeting the following two criteria:

   a. The customer would have obtained the goods and/or services from a party other than the vendor.
   b. The customer is able to reasonably estimate the fair value of the goods and/or services provided to the vendor.

   Any excess of cash consideration received by the customer over the fair value of the goods and/or services delivered to the vendor reduces the customer's cost of sales.

2. **Reimbursement of costs.** A reimbursement of the customer's specific incremental, identifiable costs incurred to sell the vendor's products or services, which is accounted for by the customer as a reduction of that cost. To the extent the cash consideration received exceeds the actual cost being reimbursed, the excess reduces cost of sales and/or inventory.

Vendors sometimes enter into binding arrangements that offer customers specified amounts of cash rebates or refunds payable in the future only if the customer remains a customer for a specified period of time, or purchases a specified cumulative dollar amount of goods or services from the vendor. In general, these arrangements are to be recorded by the customer as reductions of cost of sales by systematically allocating a portion of the benefits to be received to each transaction that results in progress toward meeting the target that results in earning the benefit. In order to use this pro rata accounting, however, the amount of the refund must be both probable and reasonably estimable. The following indicators, if present, may impair the customer's ability to determine that the refund is both probable and estimable:

1. The rebate or refund applies to purchases that are to occur over a "relatively long period" (a term undefined in the consensus)
2. An absence of historical experience with similar products or changed circumstances that make historical experience irrelevant
3. A past history of significant adjustments to expected rebates or refunds
4. Susceptibility of the product to significant external factors such as technological obsolescence or changes in demand

If the rebate or refund is not considered both probable and estimable, it is not recognized by the customer until it is fully earned by reaching the specified milestone (e.g., the dollar amount of cumulative purchases is reached or the time period for remaining a customer has expired).

Changes in a customer's estimate of the amount of future rebates or refunds and retroactive changes by a vendor to a previous offer are recognized using a "cumulative catch-up adjustment." This is accomplished by the customer's immediately charging or crediting cost of sales in an amount that will adjust the cumulative amounts recognized under the arrangement to the changed terms. Of course, if any portion of the adjustment impacts goods still in the customer's inventory, that portion would adjust the valuation of the inventory and not cost of sales.

APPLYING THE FOREGOING GUIDANCE TO SALES INCENTIVES OFFERED BY MANUFACTURERS TO CONSUMERS (EITF 03-10)

The immediately preceding discussion is applicable to situations in which cash consideration is received by a customer from a vendor, and is presumed to be a reduction of the prices of the vendor's products or services. Such incentives are to be characterized as a reduction of cost of sales when recognized in the customer's income statement. There are other instances, however, where consideration is a reimbursement for incentives offered to end users (e.g., retail customers) honored by the vendor's customer (retailer). The common example is coupons given to end users to be redeemed at the retailers offering the vendor's products for sale.

HOW TAXES COLLECTED FROM CUSTOMERS AND REMITTED TO GOVERNMENTAL AUTHORITIES SHOULD BE PRESENTED IN THE INCOME STATEMENT

When a company collects taxes from customers on behalf of government authorities, it may report these taxes either on a gross basis (included in revenues and costs) or on a net basis (excluded from revenues). If it elects to report on a gross basis, then it should disclose the amounts of those taxes in interim and annual financial statements if the amounts are significant.

INDEX